Glenn Sorensen

Glenn Sorensen

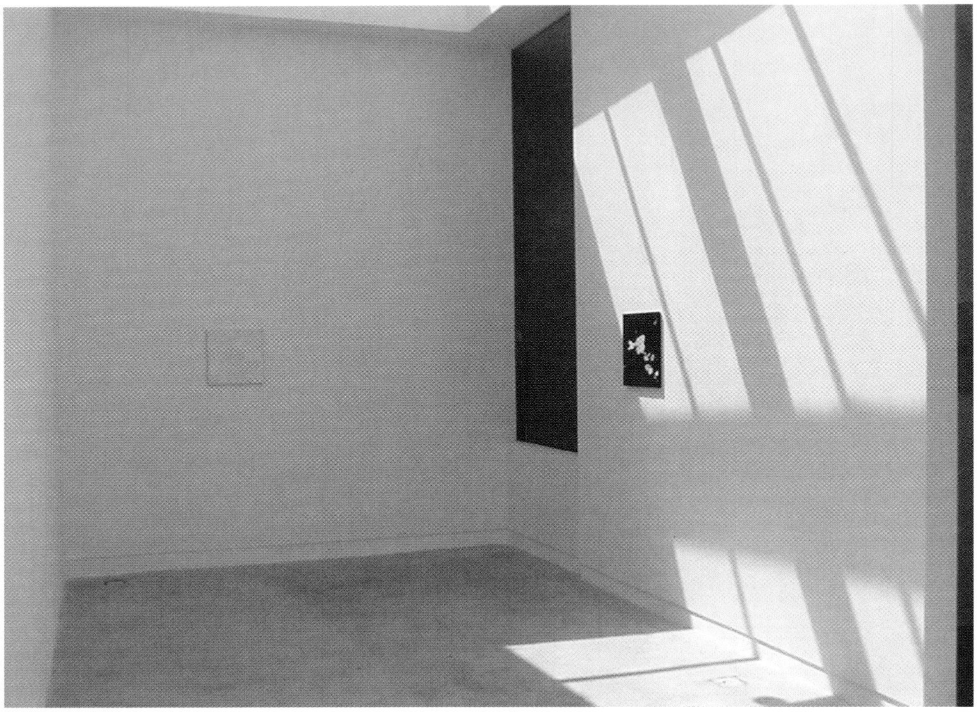

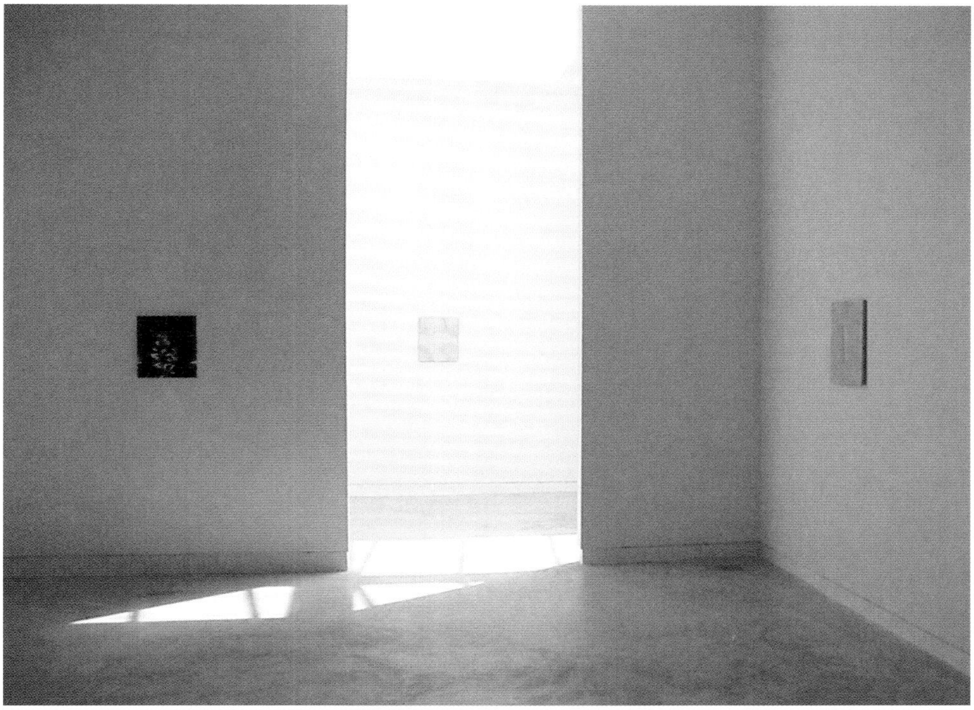

I was having dinner at a friend's house recently when I noticed a new painting on the wall. It was a strange, unassuming little image called **Cigarette Plant** by Glenn Sorensen and, although it had taken me a while to register its presence, once I had, it stayed with me. The painting depicts, against a dark background, a delicate green plant which appears to be lit by a strangely uneven light. Numerous cigarettes are perched, for no apparent reason, on its leaves. The paint looks as if it were applied to the canvas with a kind of grubby, but somehow heartfelt, diligence. The drawing is a little awkward, the palette dark and artificial, the mood slightly trippy but understated. It was, in fact, the perfect complement to my mood that night – I was tired and slightly drunk, and my mind was wandering from subject to subject in a lazy, odd-connection kind of way. I was also really enjoying smoking. So were my friends. I think it was Kafka who observed that a blind man would have no reason to smoke because one of the main pleasures it affords is visual: dissolving gently in front of you, the smoke softens hard lines, casting a faint veil around you as it disappears, weaving through atmospheres and imaginations with intimations of fire. But, despite the enjoyment and relaxation smoking can generate, as you inhale it is impossible to entirely reject the nagging, negative thoughts festering at the back of your mind about the harm you might be doing to your body. Smoking is endlessly appealing in the way some damaging relationships can be appealing, the danger of the interaction fuelling the flames of the attraction. Maybe this accounts for the slightly polluted ambiguity of **Cigarette Plant** – that the flip side to pleasure is the imminent melancholy of either its passing, or ill effects.

So, during the dinner at my friend's house, my gaze kept returning to Sorensen's painting. The background is black but not a night-black – it's too impenetrable for that, like an upright backdrop, not something you could walk over or through. The cigarettes balance impossibly on the leaves of the plant. They are humble little shapes, unpretentious objects of comfort, not harbingers of doom. But despite the surreal quality of the image, it is pervaded with an aura of gentle, quite real, melancholy, which, I discovered, is a common denominator in many of Sorensen's paintings, even though they are not painted as a group or a series. Things and ideas – a patterned fabric; flowers floating in front of a window; the shape of an ashtray or a cigarette; the smooth surface of a telephone; the way a girl's hand drops when she's asleep on the couch – connect his pictures but in a modest, slightly oblique way, like a group of silent people on a bus, linked not because of who they are but because of their shared destination and immediate environment. Cigarettes, for example, are made from the tobacco plant, but the title of the painting – **Cigarette Plant** – is like the idea of cigarettes planting in your mind and growing there until you work out your relationship with them.

I like looking at pictures in homes – they're the best place for reverie, or puffing quietly on a cigarette while you watch the smoke curl up to a familiar ceiling while you concentrate on a small detail of your day or surroundings; a place where, if you wish, you can gaze at nothing, until the need for gazing overcomes you; a sanctuary where you can drink a glass of wine alone and unobserved and sigh out loud as another day recedes; the only place where every image you look at is something you **choose** to look at. You should never feel self-conscious in your home. When you go to a gallery, you are there specifically to look at art. In a home, you need only look at pictures when you feel the urge. A sudden openness to examining, or making, an image can happen at the most unexpected of moments: when you're lying on a bed, half asleep; eating a meal; taking a bath or drowsily walking down a corridor.

The images that preoccupy Sorensen appear to be almost exclusively inspired by the activities you do at home. That said, his paintings aren't so much about simply recreating or illustrating the domestic sphere as using it as a springboard to create a visual vocabulary that meanders and leaps. For example, watching a TV programme, the artist might see a pattern on an actress' dress that becomes a painting that has no obvious bearing on the initial subject-matter; a friend might tell him a story that fuses with his own stories to become a single image; a bunch of flowers might become a starting point to explore a colour sequence; a round ashtray might become the almost-abstracted component of what might initially look like a colour field painting that's been left out in the rain and had half of its paint washed away. Odd interruptions occur, such as in the few paintings which feature a hummingbird, forever stilled in the process of getting nectar from a flower. The birds in these paintings look more like the idea of birds than actual birds; blurred representations of permanent deferral. Like smoke, the paint in Sorensen's paintings tends to dissolve at the edges. Without being ugly or obvious, his palette reminds me of the colours of decay or bruising or nostalgia – blacks, purples, greens, browns, mauves, pinks. I assume that when he paints it's usually in the late afternoon, or the evening of a grey day, and that his studio isn't that well lit. I know it's an absurd assumption, but somehow these images make me think like that. It's as if the environments or states of mind that I guess influenced them have seeped onto their surfaces.

All of Sorensen's paintings are small, which is totally in keeping with their intensity and intimacy. Looking at a small painting is somehow a more private experience than looking at a big one – you have to lean into them and look closely at their surface, even breathe them in to see them properly. The portraits are particularly suited to such a scale. Looking at them is like glimpsing, for a moment and from a distance, perhaps through a partly opened curtain, someone absorbed in their world, imagining themselves alone. Any bigger and the subject matter might appear overblown – small, these glimpses of other people's lives is intriguing, even touching, in their restraint.

Flowers figure prominently in Sorensen's paintings but it's hard to tell whether they're 'real' flowers, or flowers which have already been represented – for example, on wallpaper or dress material or posters. But whatever the source of their imagery, their soft-focused beauty is countered by signs of the artist's almost obsessive interest in the infinite potential of patterns and repetitions in these familiar, lovely things, as if they're asking you to realise how hard you need to work to see a flower with fresh eyes. Ultimately, of course, it doesn't matter what their source material is, and when cigarettes or faces begin to float among the petals, or form patterns amidst the blooms, a kind of gentle hallucination begins to occur that encourages you to toss all logic out the window. It's a leap of faith that is encouraged in the titles – in one painting, a pale mauve wreath of flowers is titled **Drive Carefully**, while another, which depicts overblown flowers floating in an inky expanse, is titled **She Talks in her Sleep**.

Maybe the relationship Sorensen explores between the home and looking is why I like his paintings. Sometimes they remind me of fragments of faded wallpaper or loving copies of details of Monet posters; sometimes like vague approximations of either despondency or delight. There's something so casual about his paint application, but so considered in his choice of subject matter, that their mood, apart from their definite introspective quality, is hard to pin down. That painting is a struggle is evident in the awkwardness of the drawing, but it's not an haphazard awkwardness – more like the kind of clumsiness that happens when you're really trying to come to terms with something. They're in no way neutral (which is impossible anyway in a painting), but they don't shout at you. They're like the pictures that might occur to you when you're not trying to think about anything, when your mind and eye wander about before settling on an insignificant detail which suddenly assumes a profound importance – images bled from chance encounters with the things you know.

**Jennifer Higgie**

Cigarette Plant, 1999

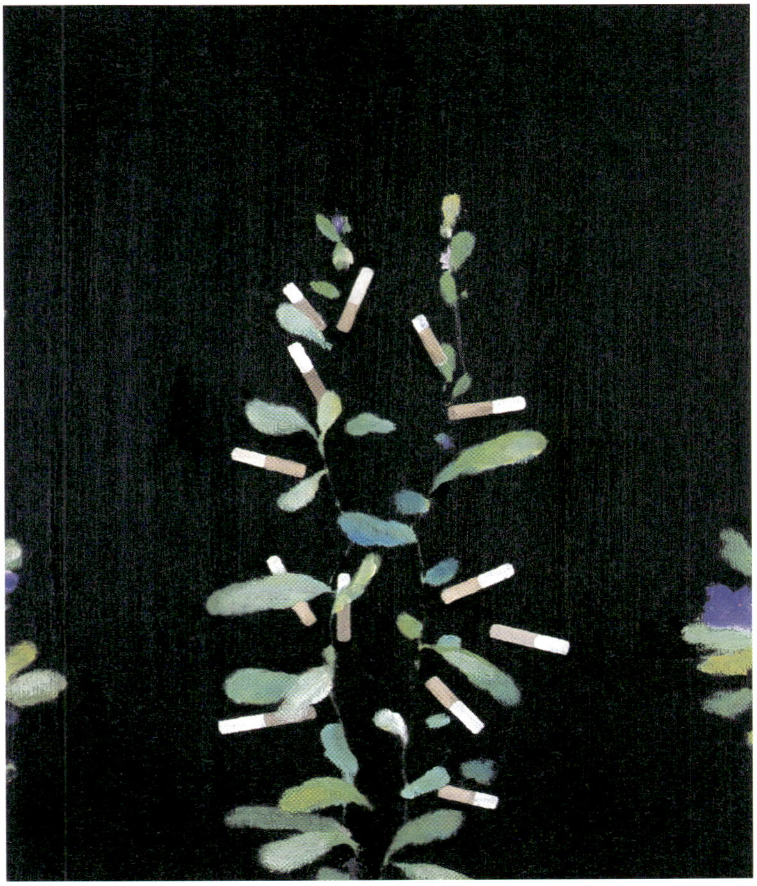

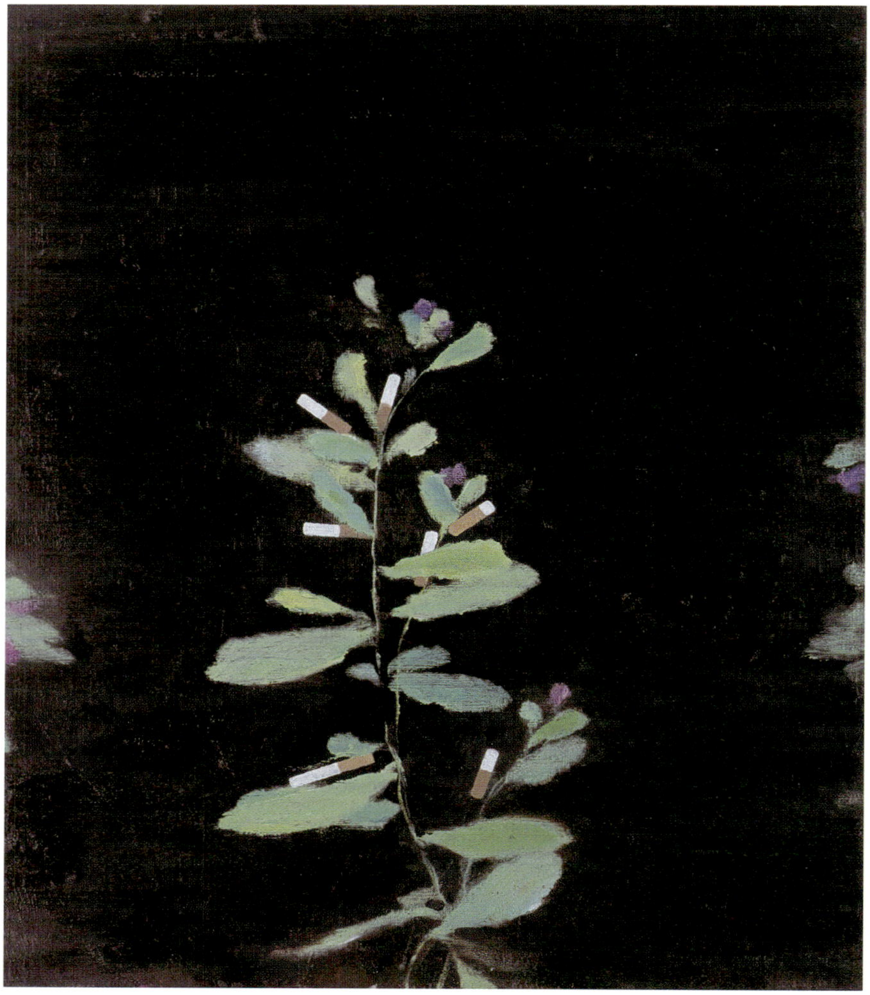

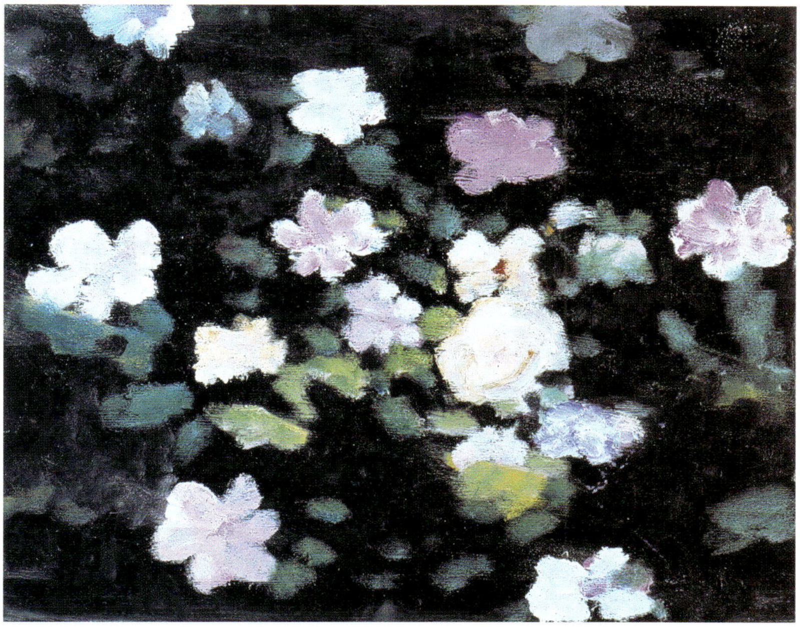

Cigarette Plant, 1999

Flowers, 1998

She Talks in her Sleep, 1998-99

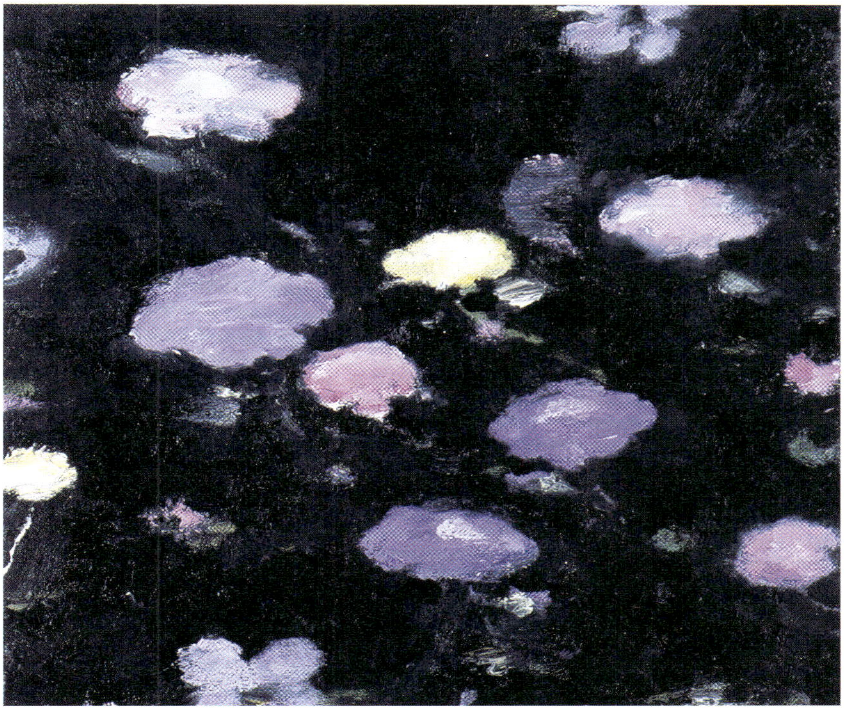

You're the Only One, 2000

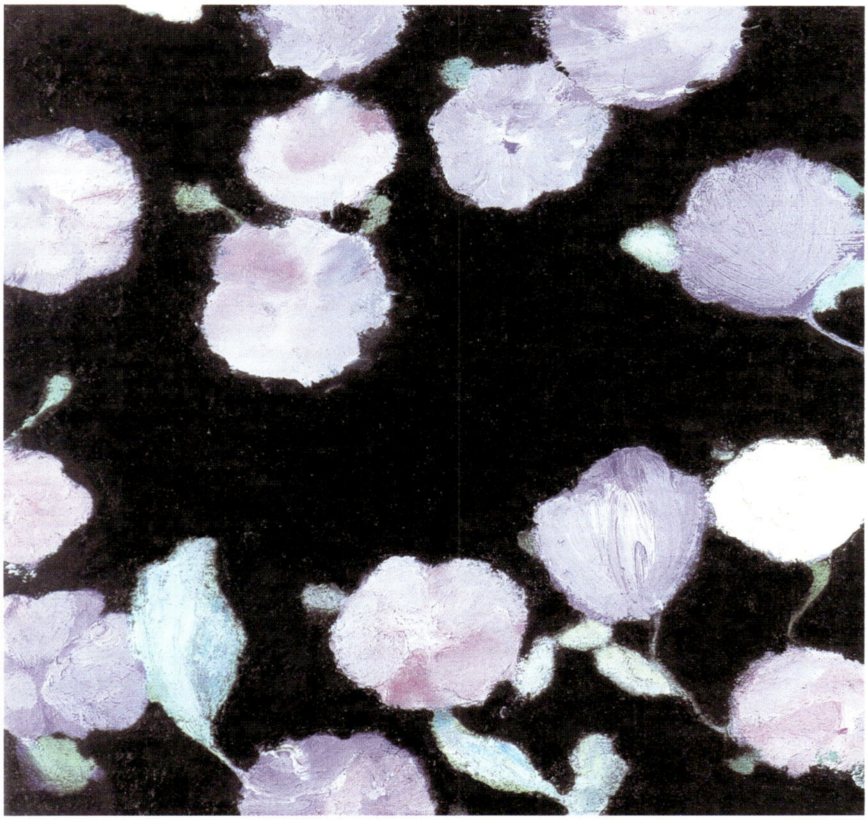

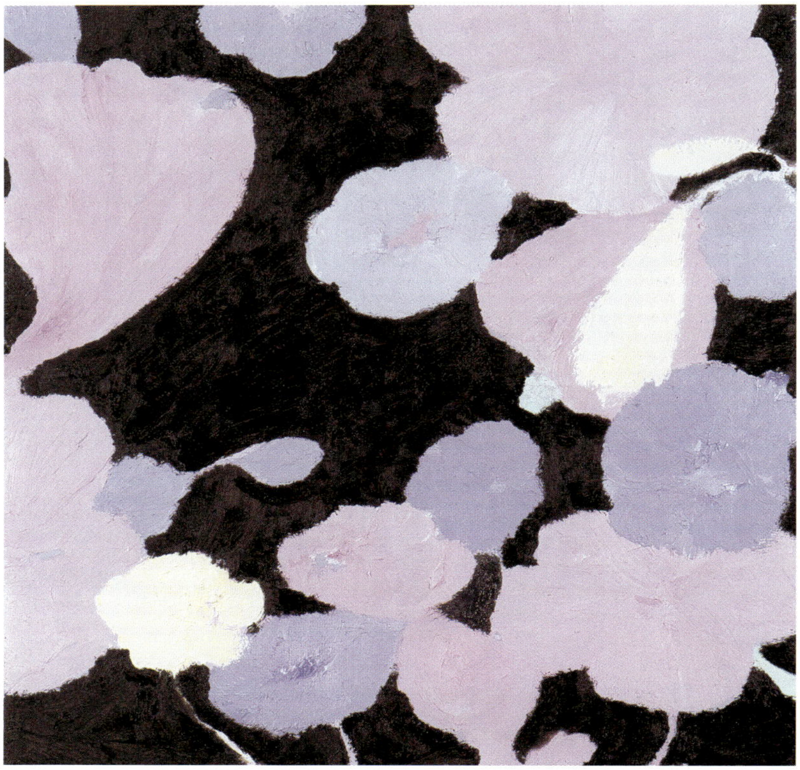

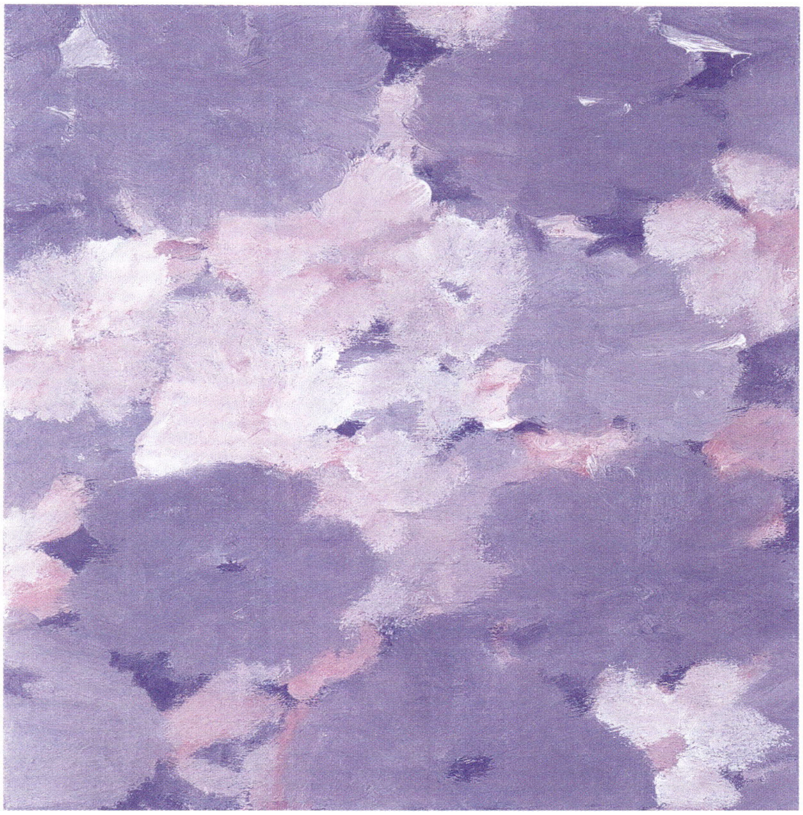

Jean, 2000

Purple Effect, 1999

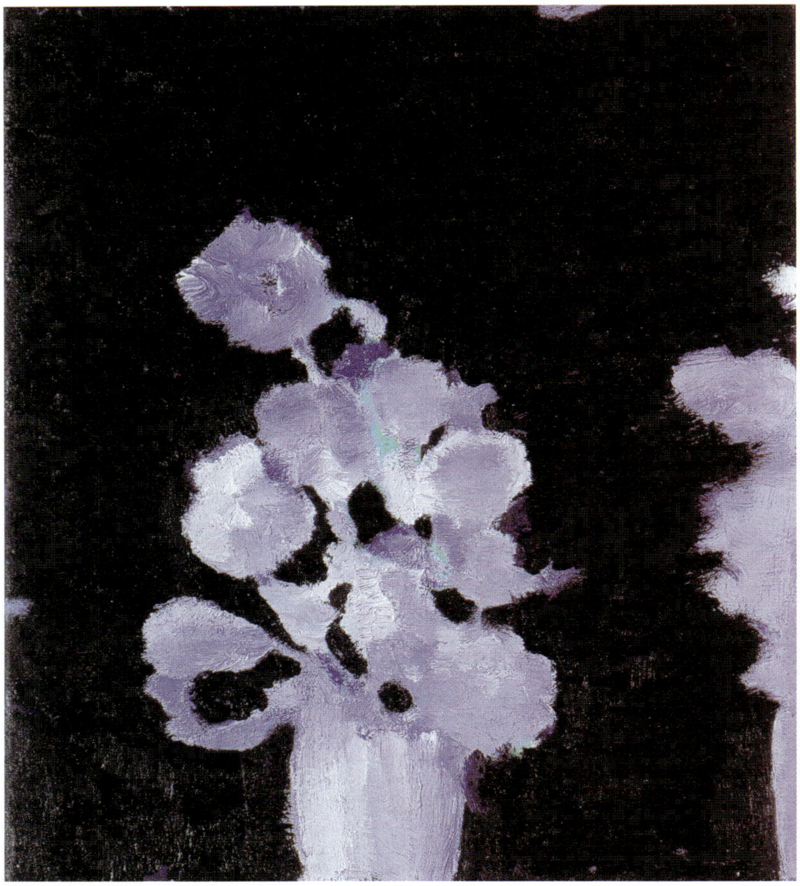

Chrysanthemums, 2000



Drive Carefully Darling, 2000

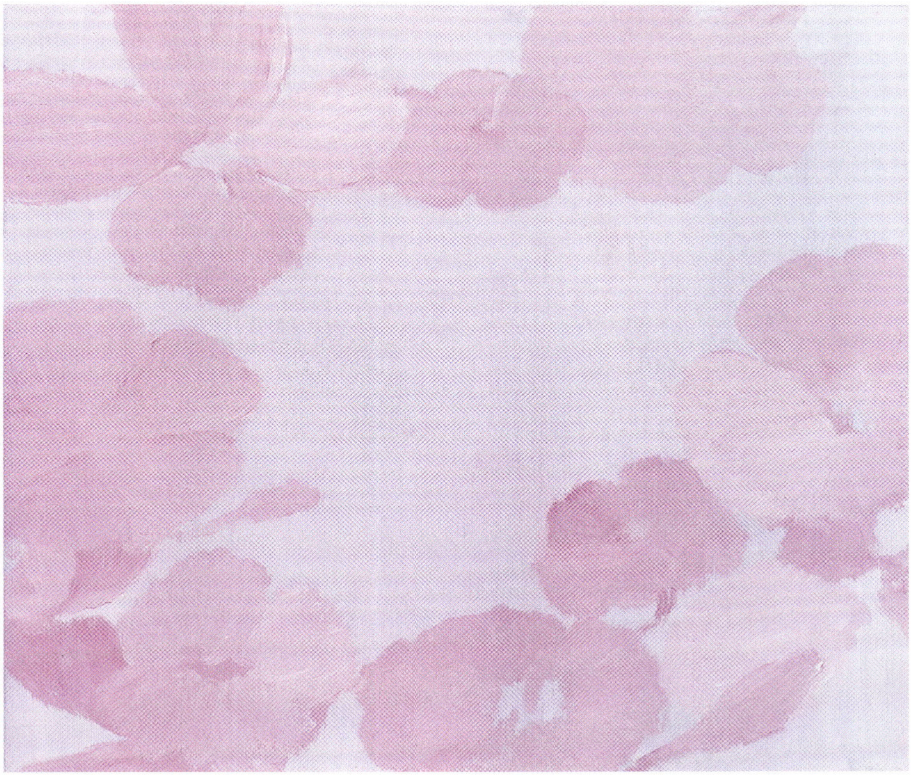

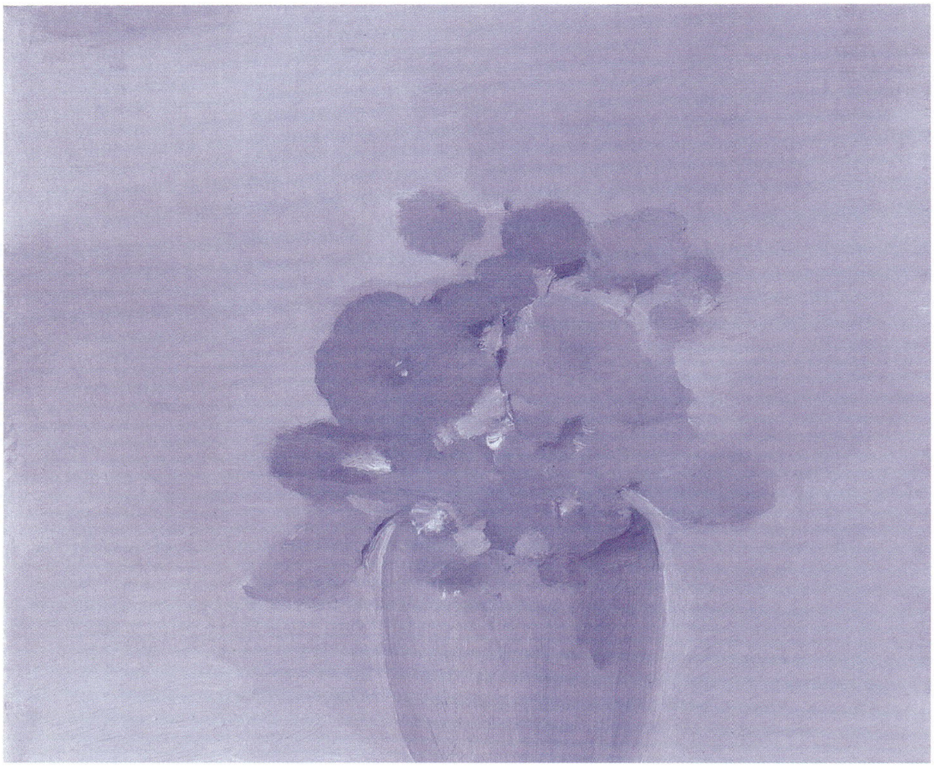



Purple Vase of Flowers, 2000

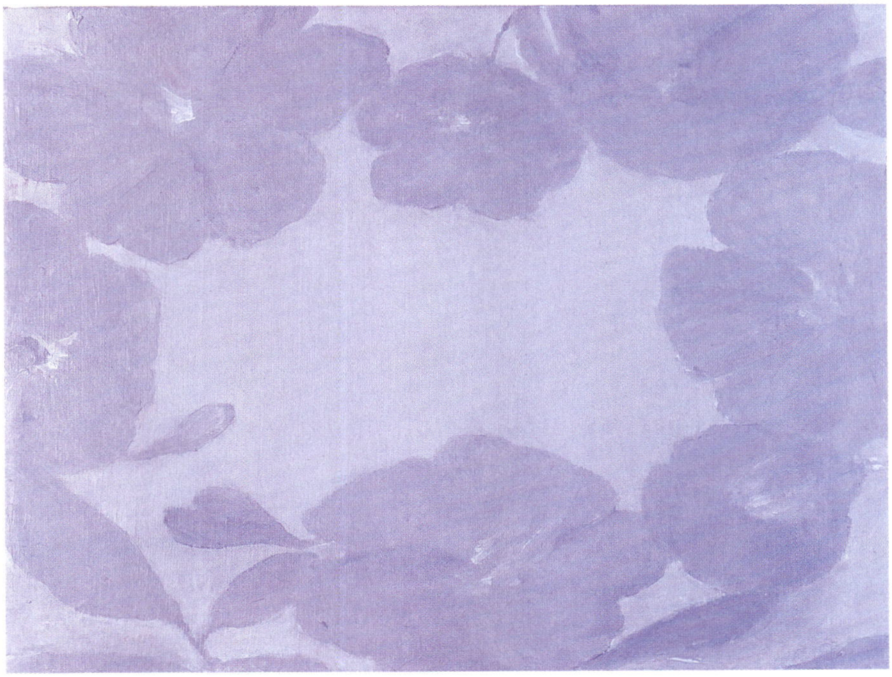

Drive Carefully, 1999

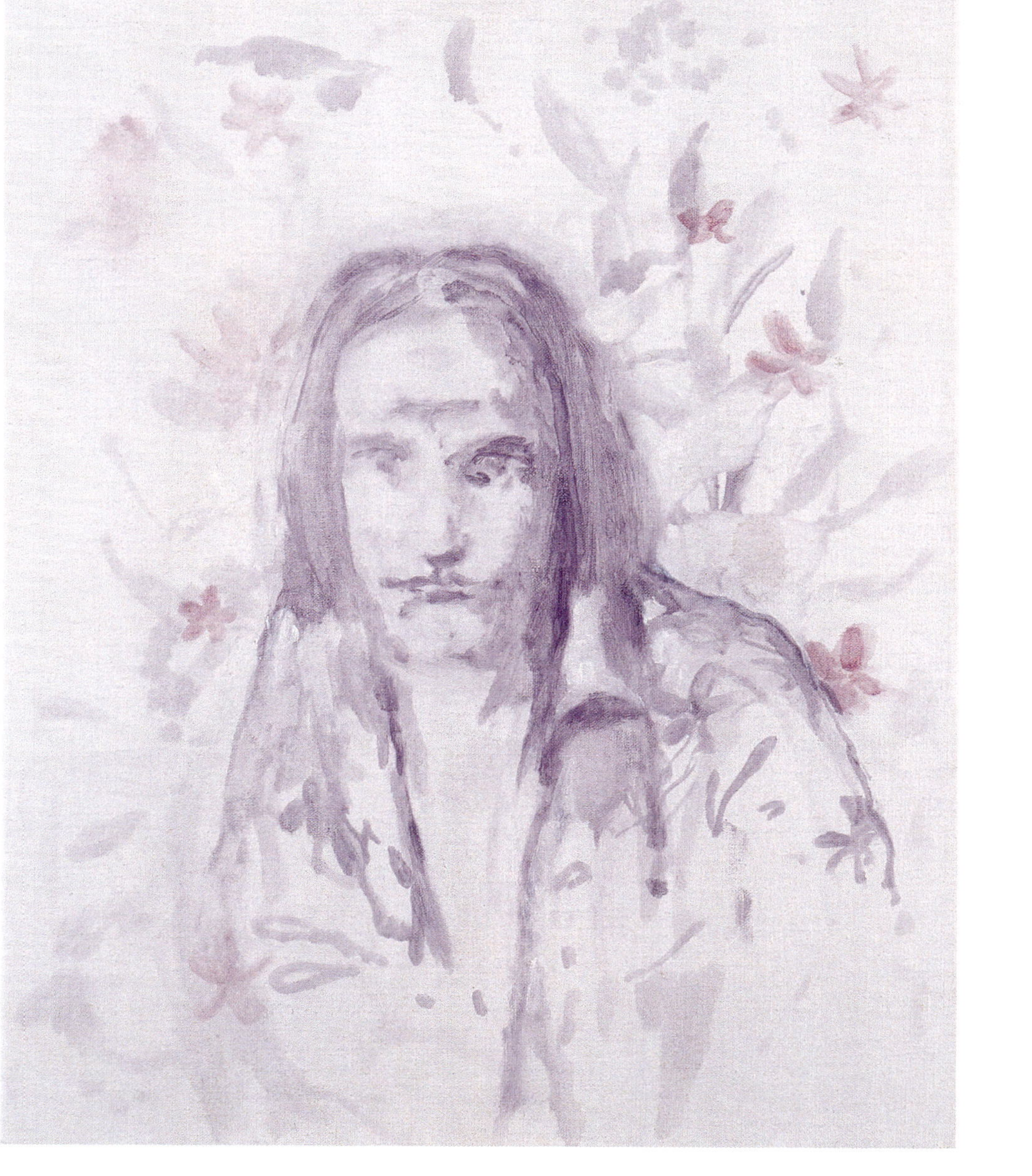



Self-Portrait, 1998

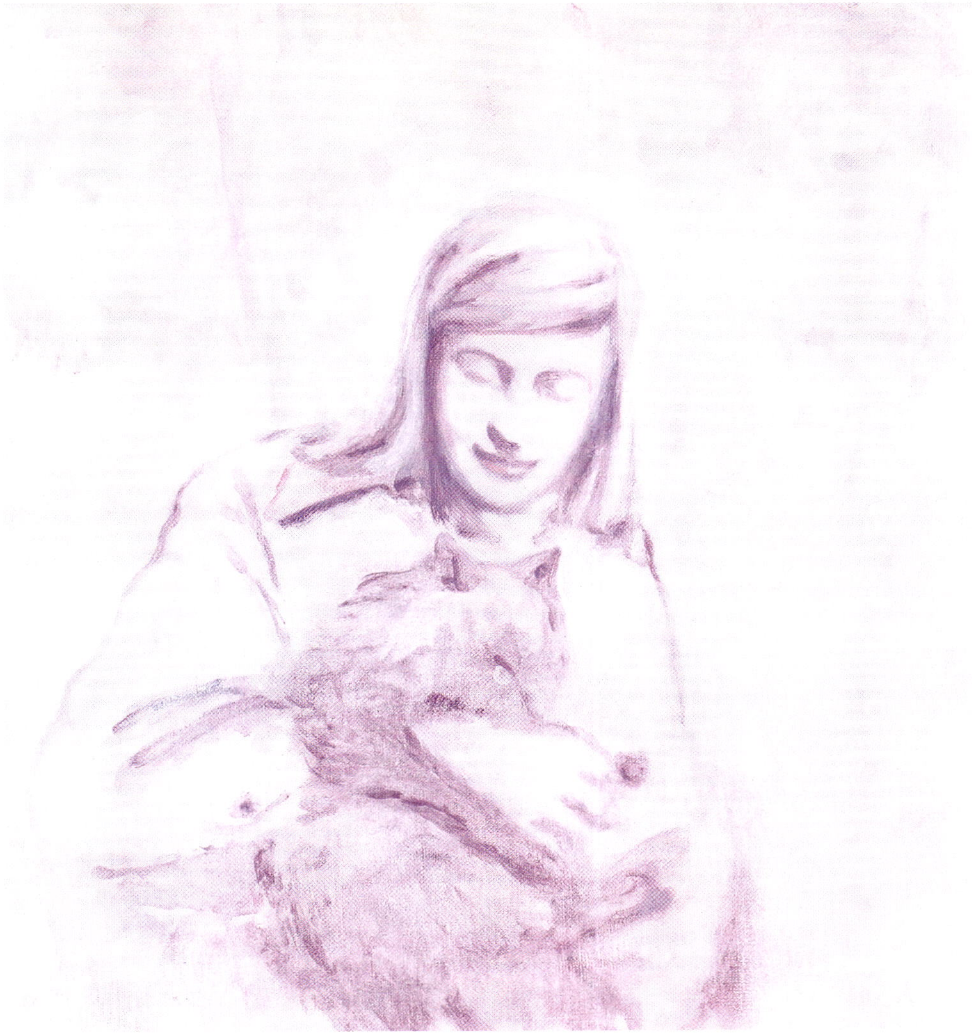

Anna, 1998

Waterfall, 2000

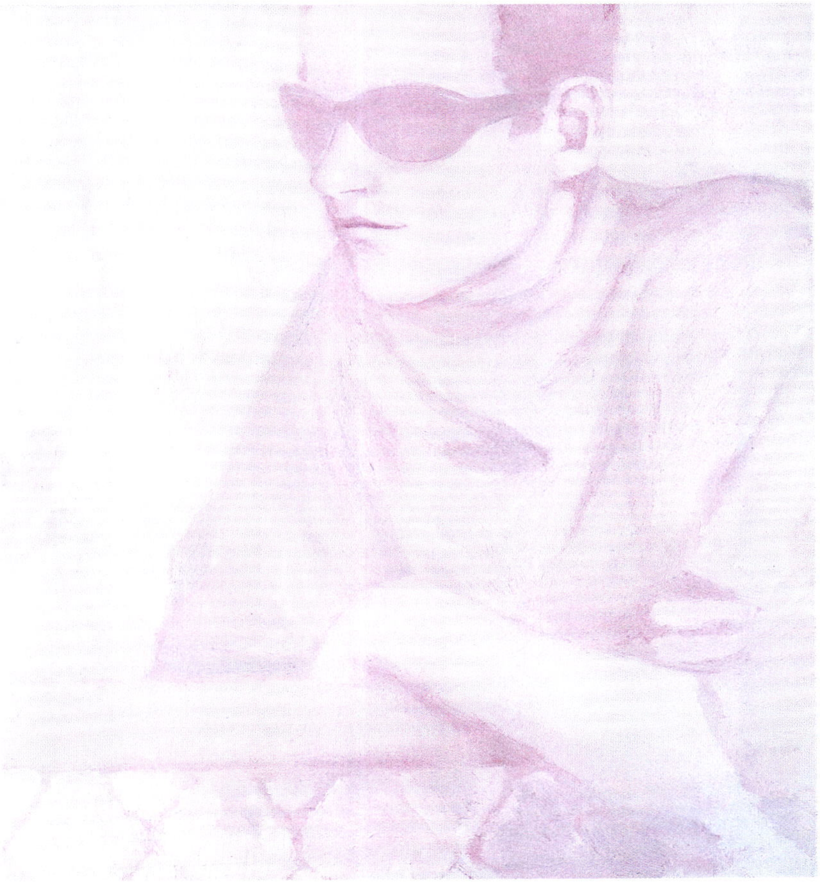

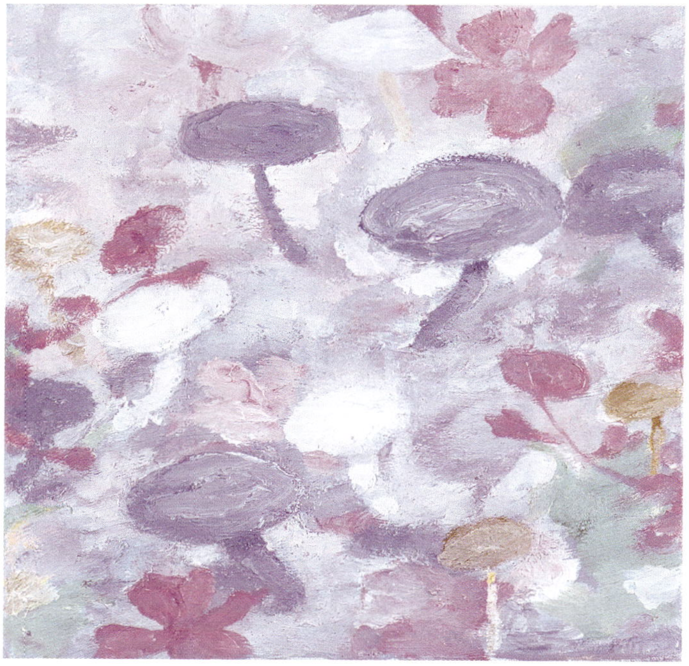

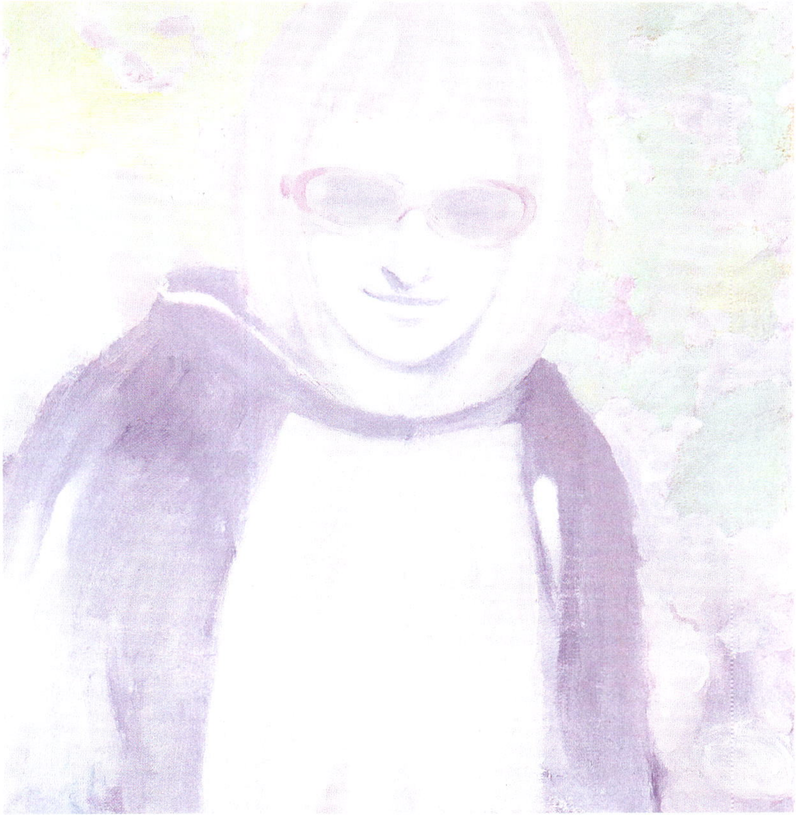

Mushrooms, 1998-99

Anna, 2000

Mauve Phone, 2000

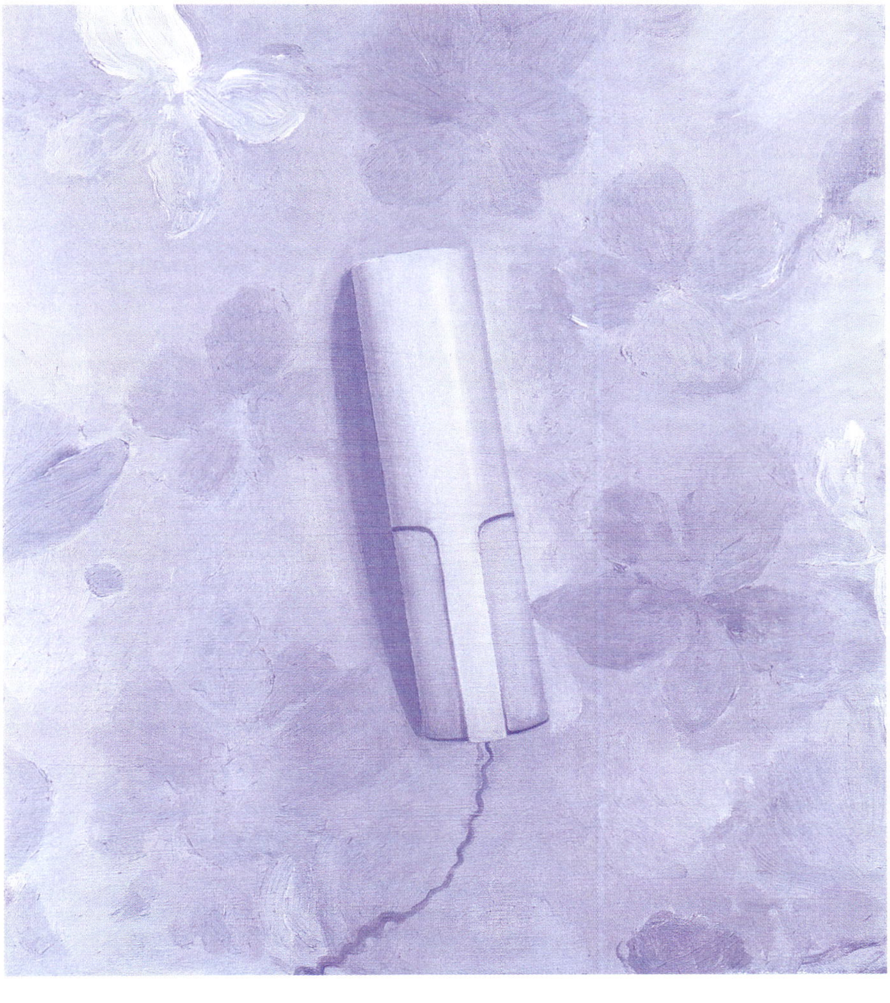

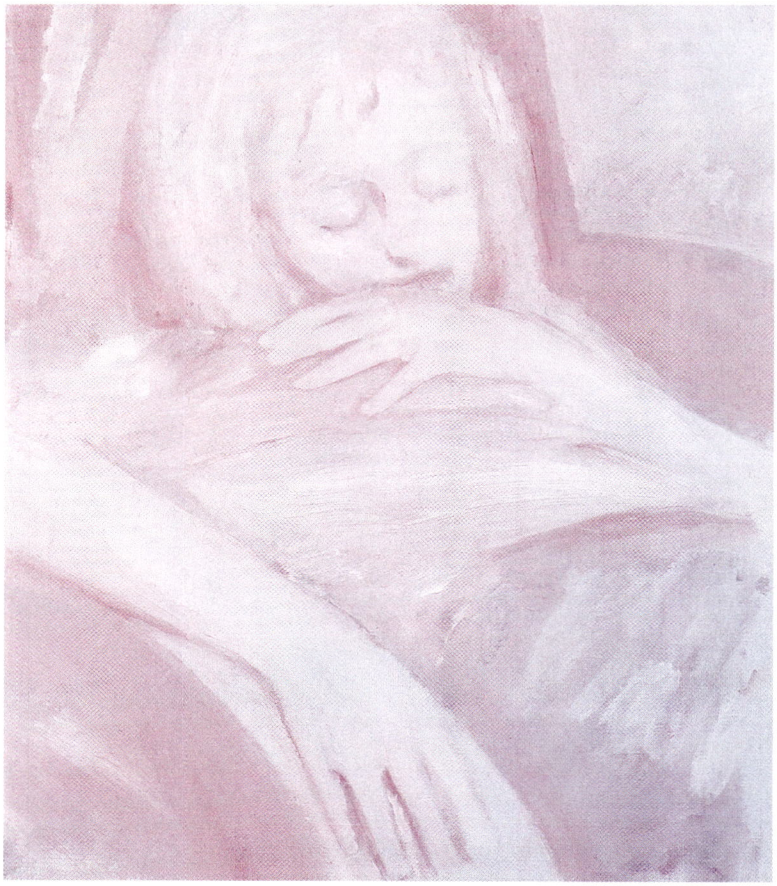

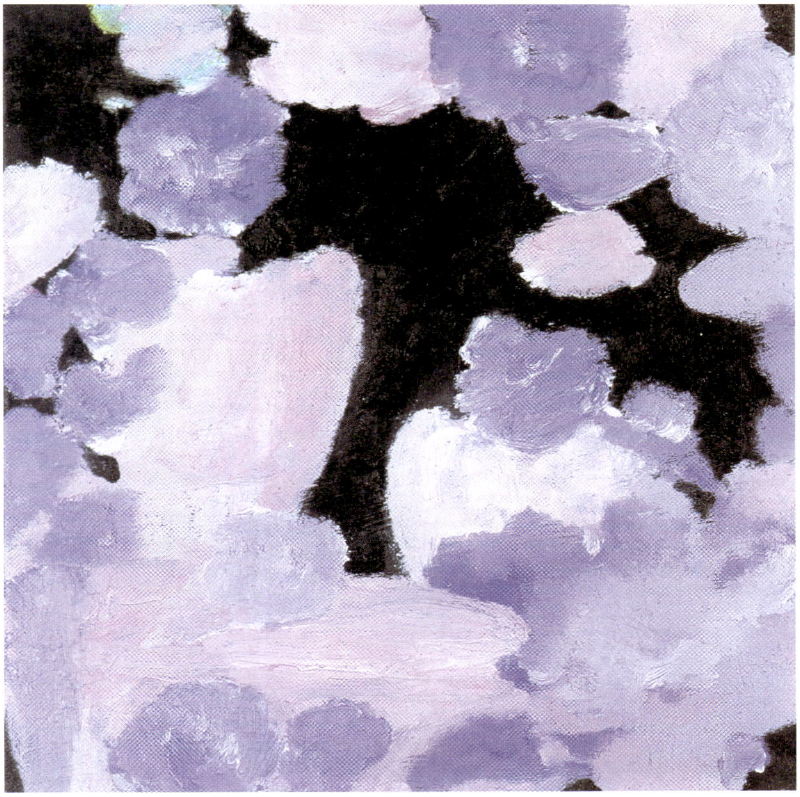

Asleep in Front of Television, 2000

All Night Every Night, 2000

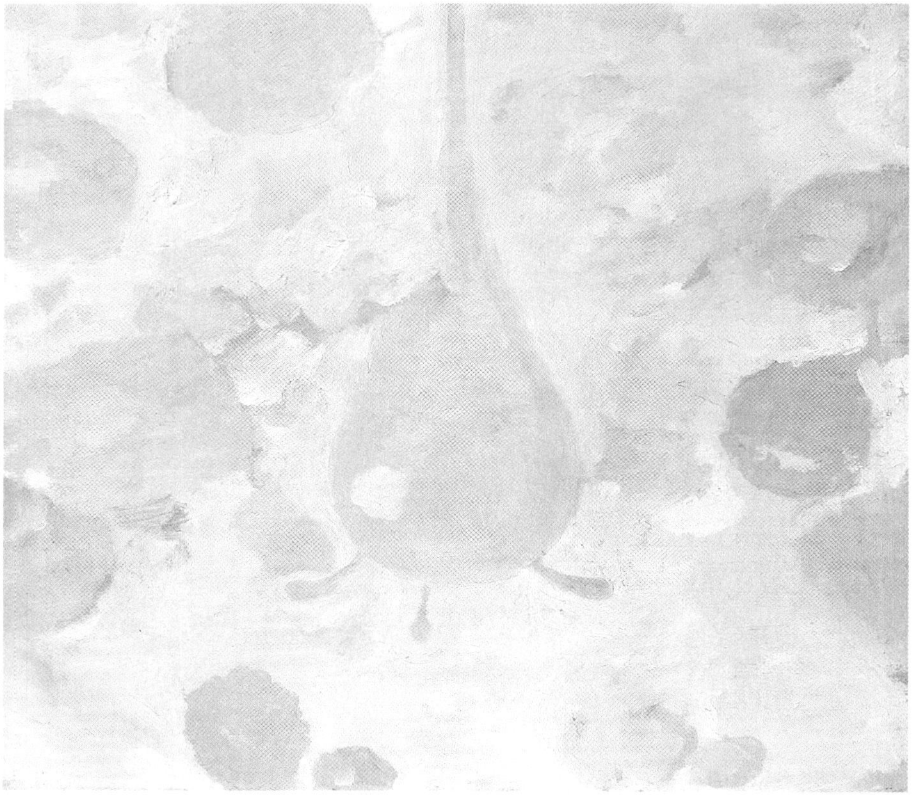



Feeder, 2000

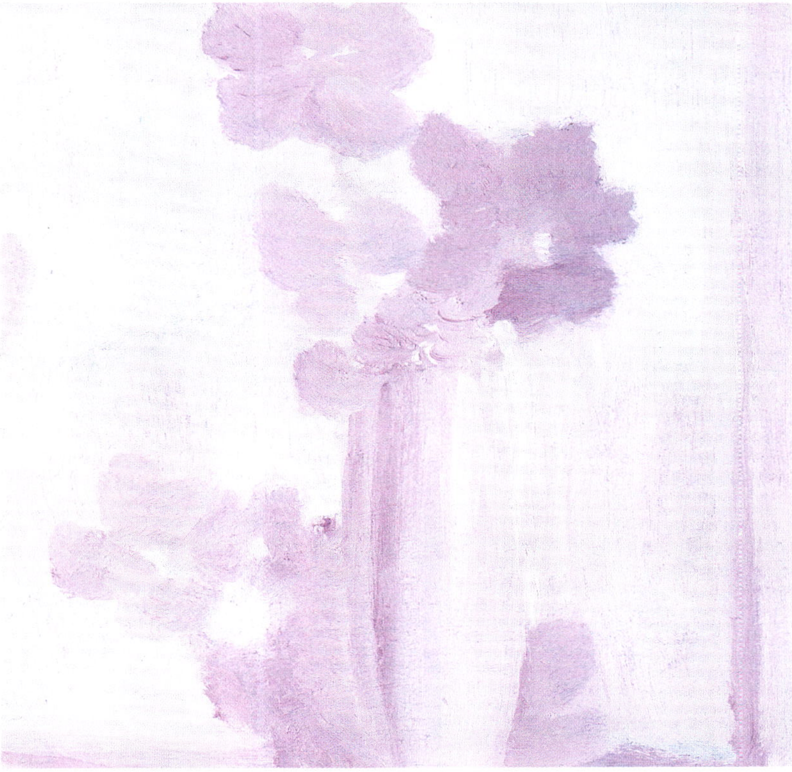

Hibiscuses, 2000

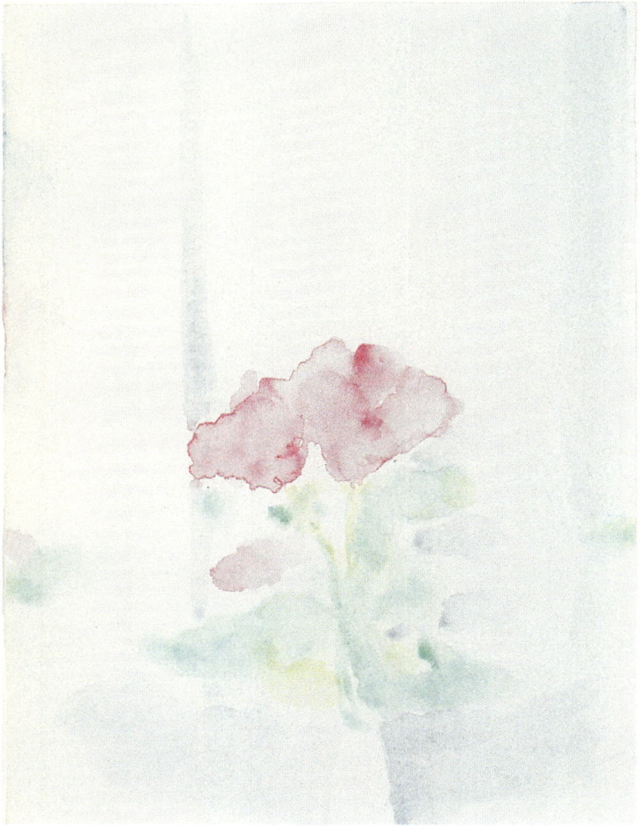

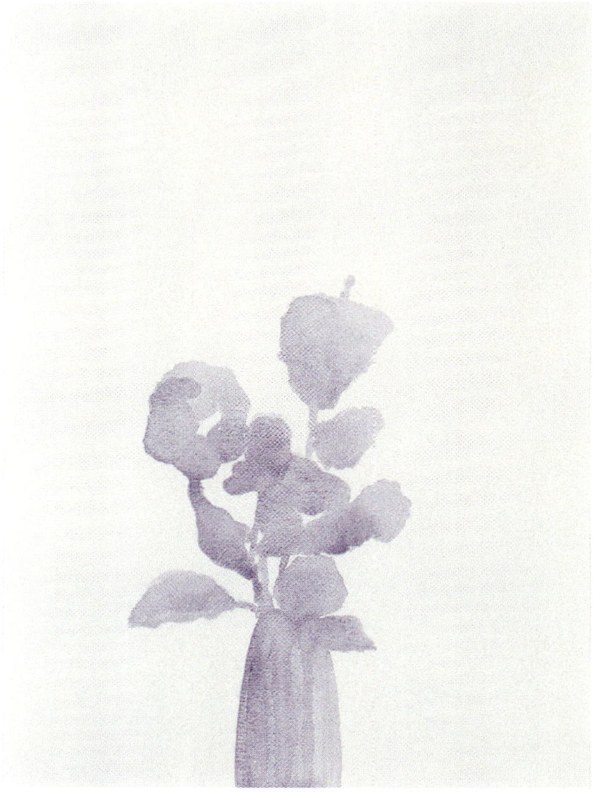

Pelargoniums, 2000

Hibiscuses, 2000

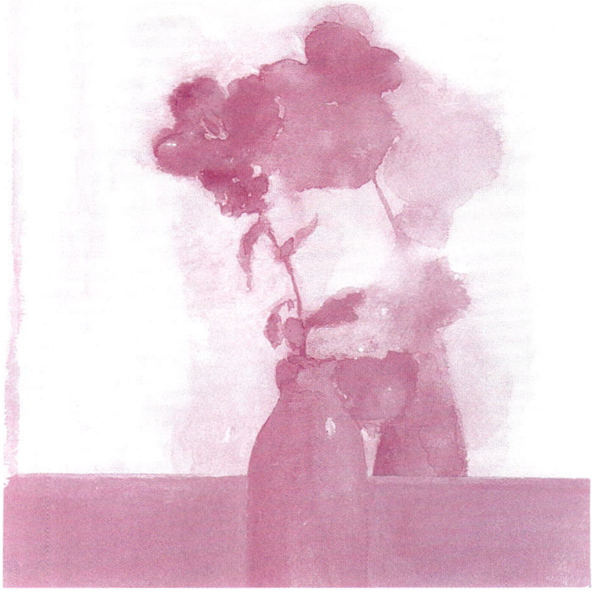

Pelargoniums, 2000

Hibiscus-mirror, 2000

Pink Hummingbirds, 1999

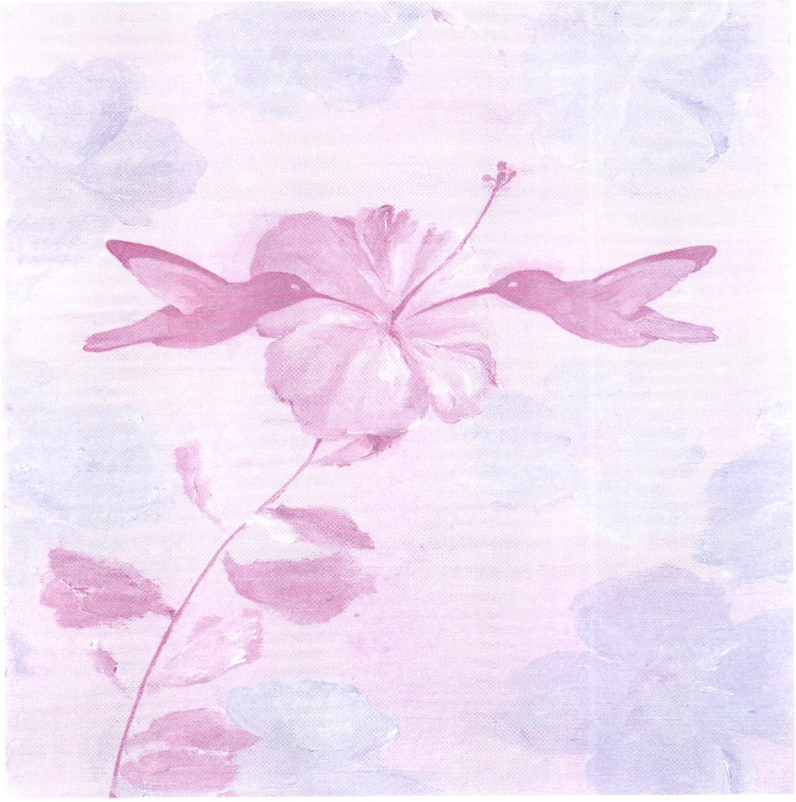

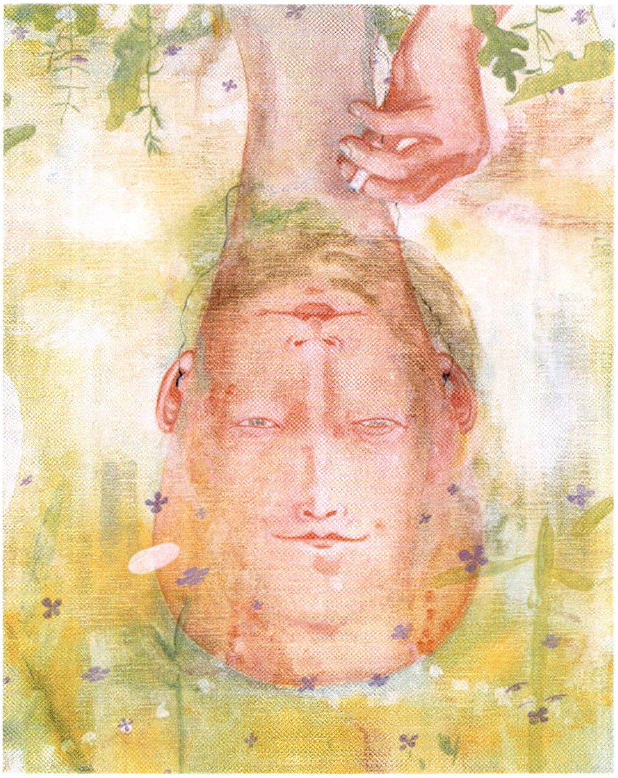

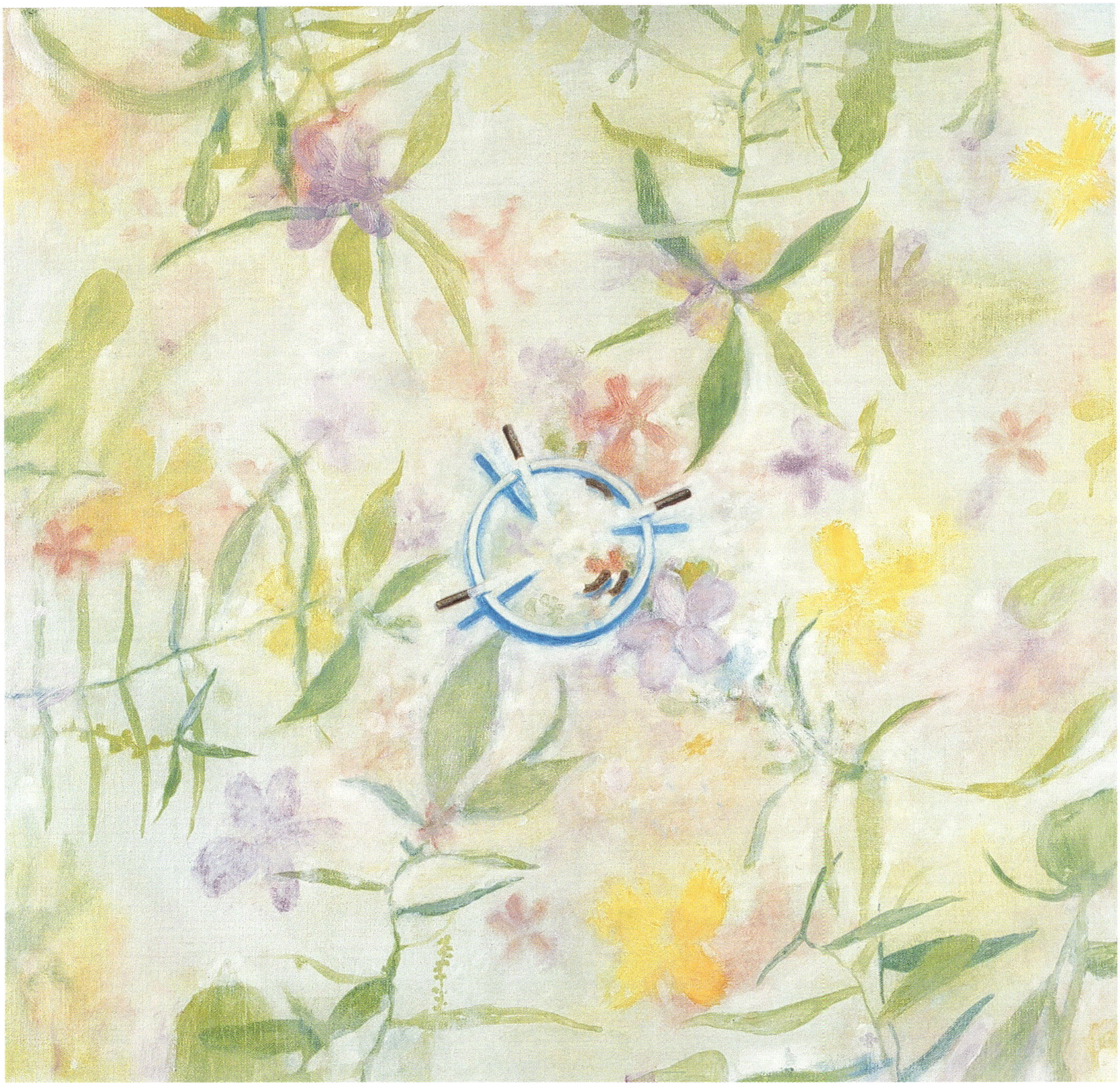



Ashtray 1/2, 1997-98

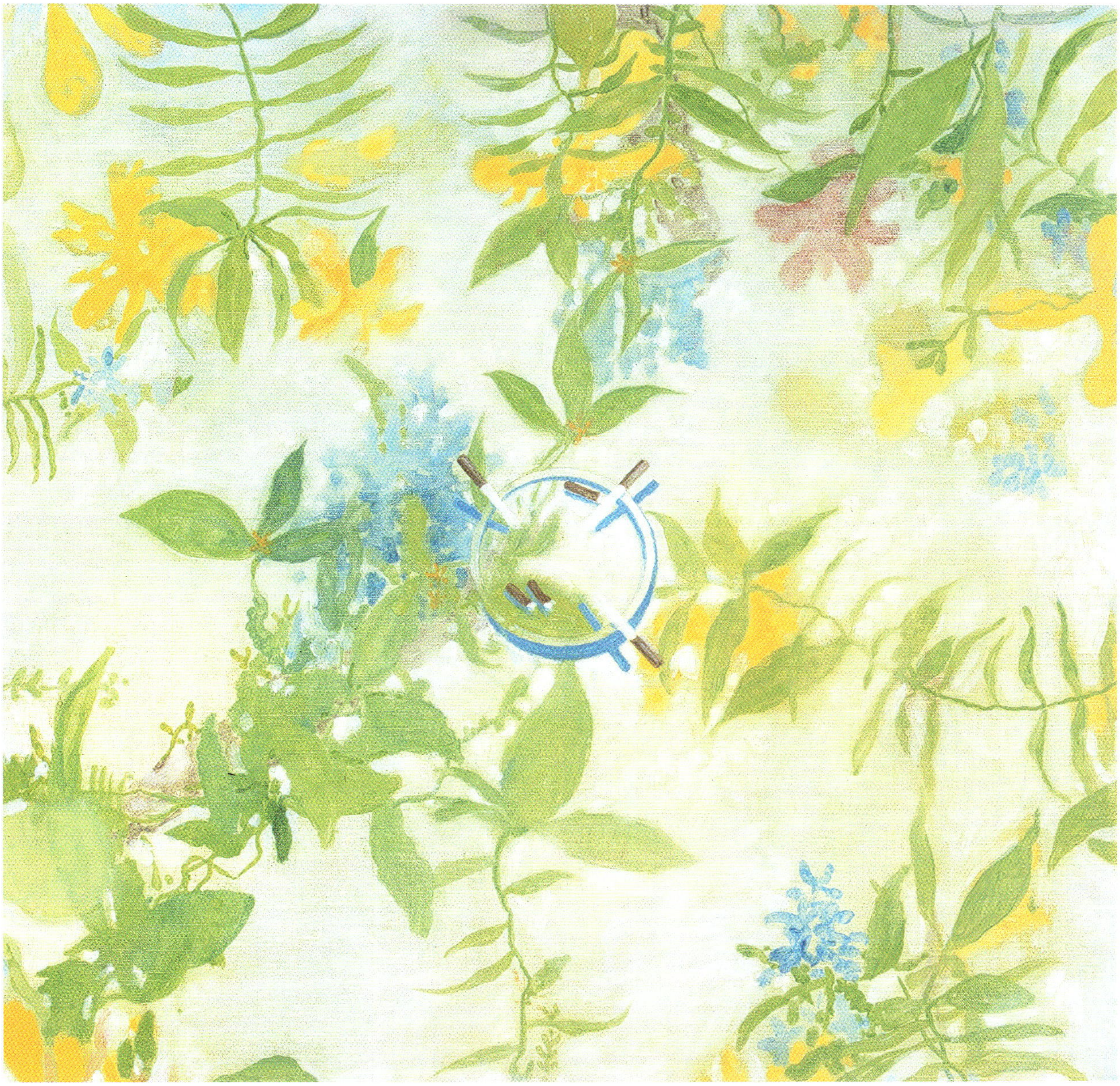

Ashtray 2/2, 1997

Four Ashtrays, 1998-99

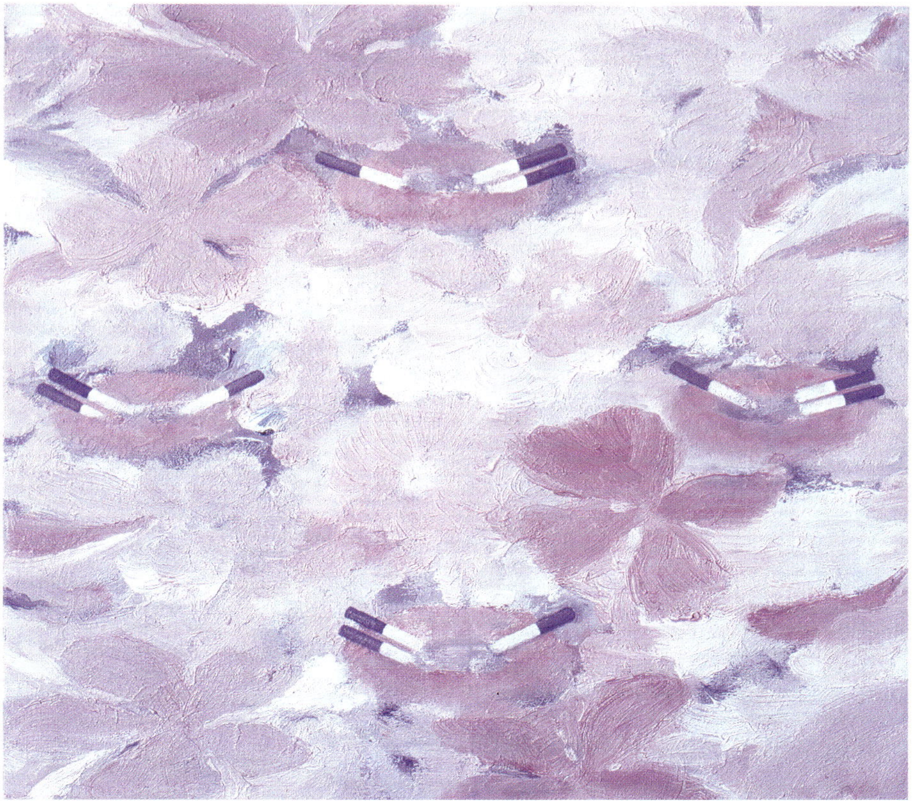

Hummingbirds and Ashtrays, installation view, 2000

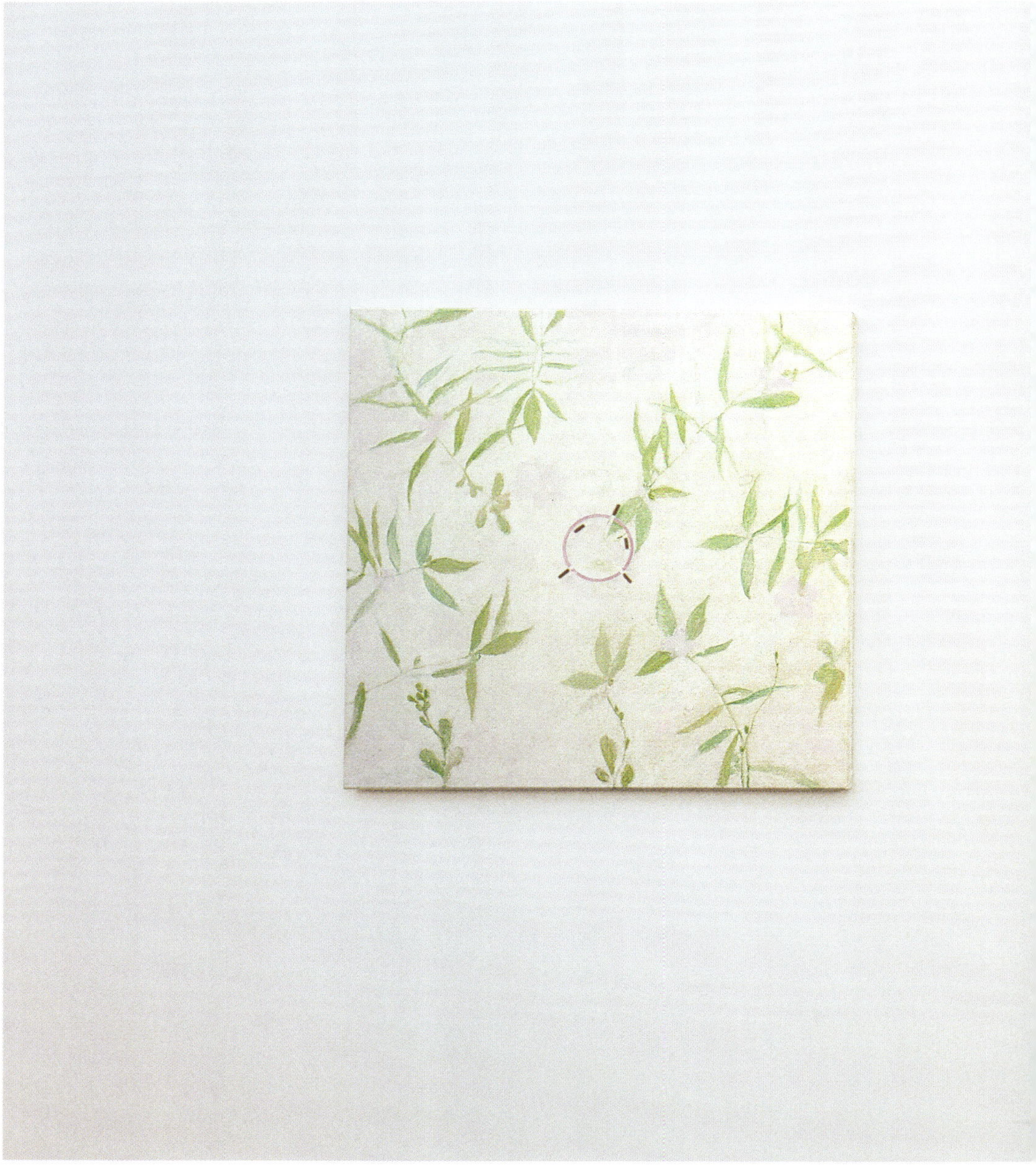

Ashtrays, installation view, 1999

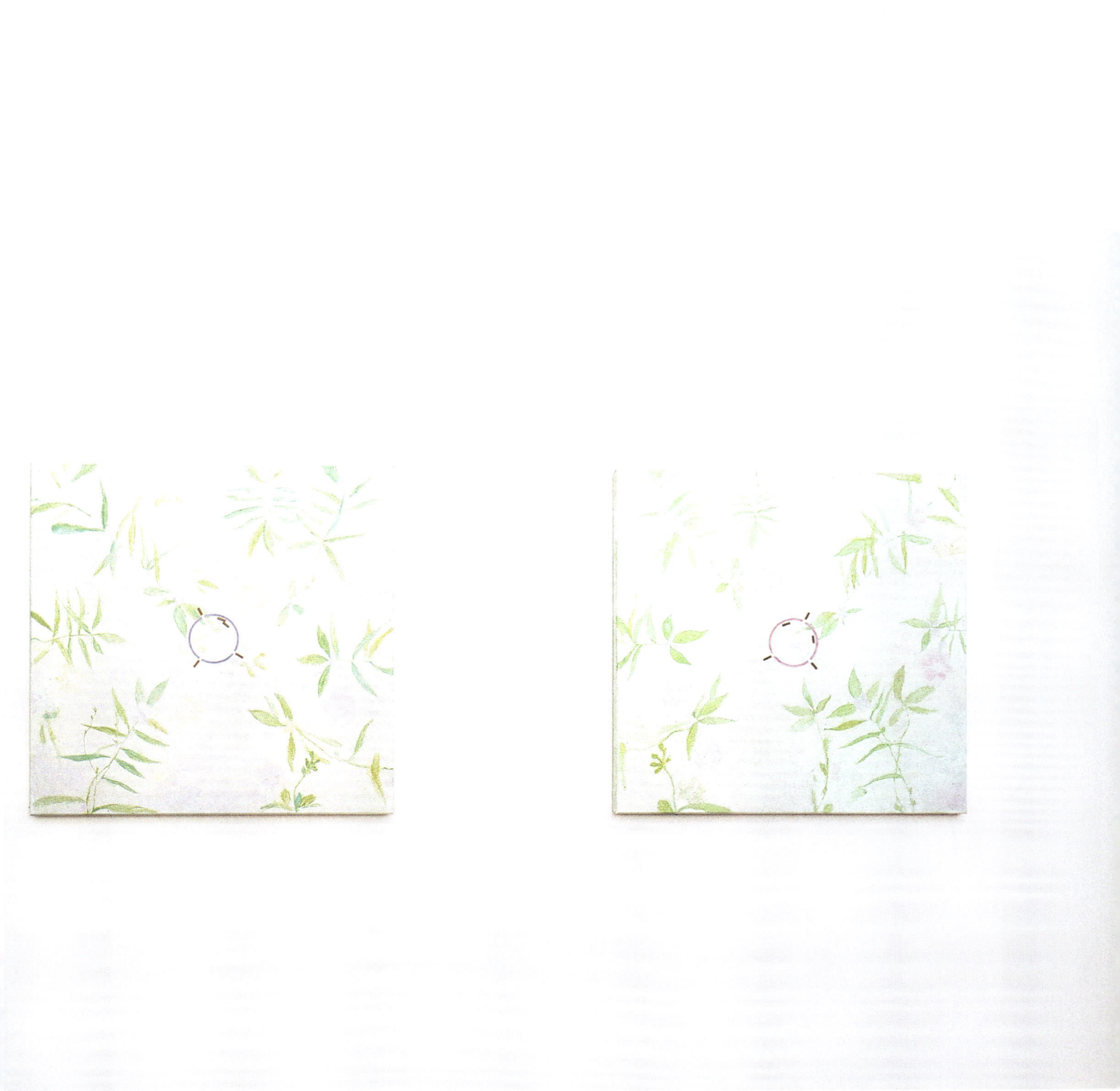

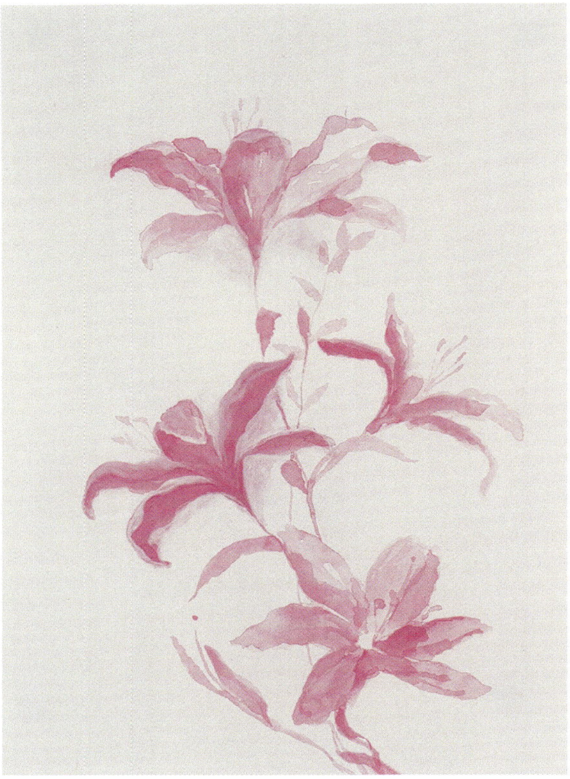

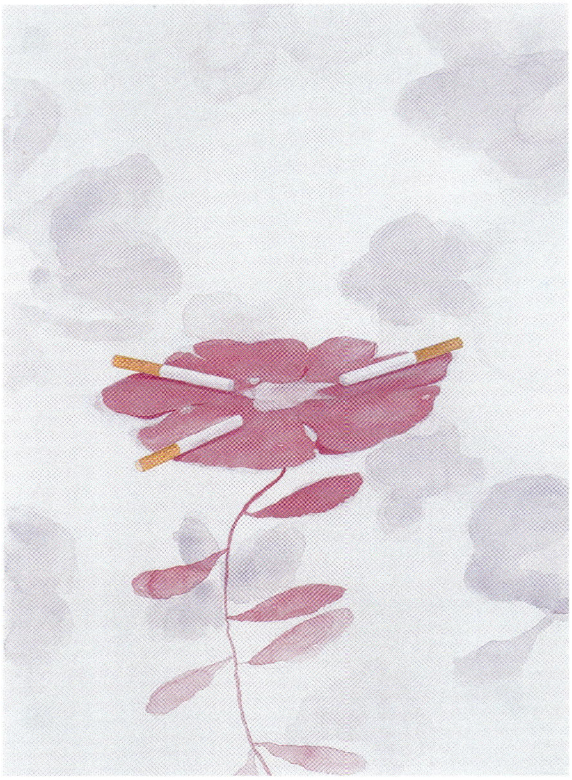

My Mother-in-law's Flowers, 1999

Flower and Cigarettes, 1999

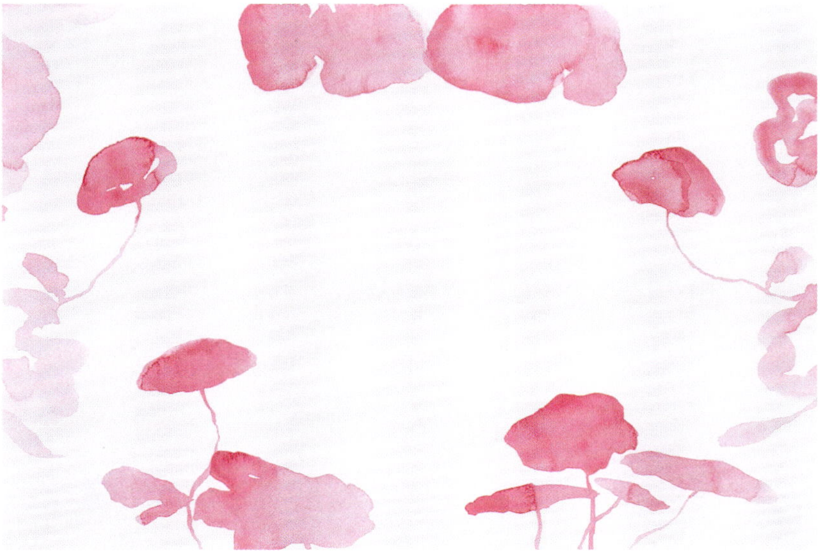

Flowers, 1999

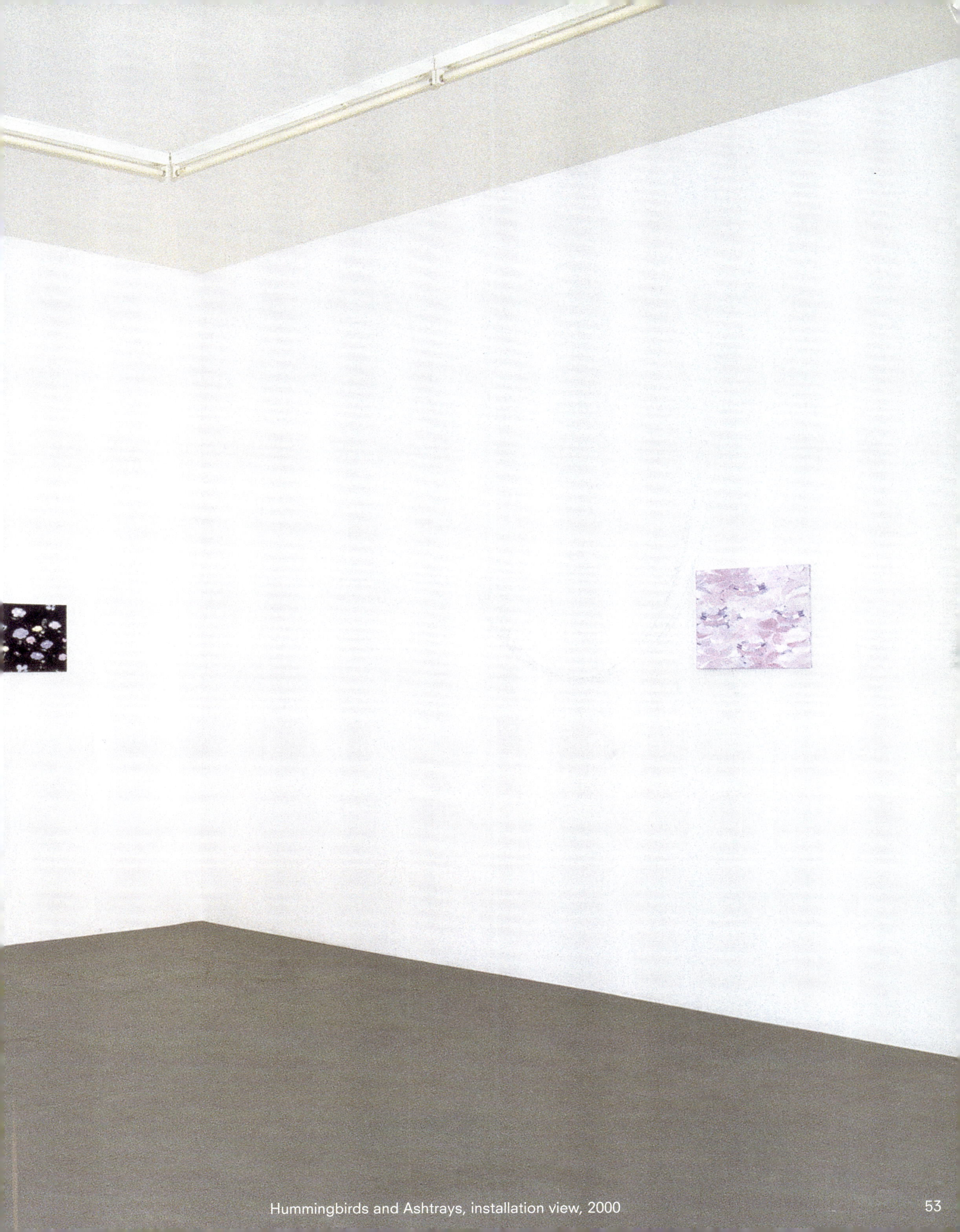

Hummingbirds and Ashtrays, installation view, 2000

Hummingbird, 1999

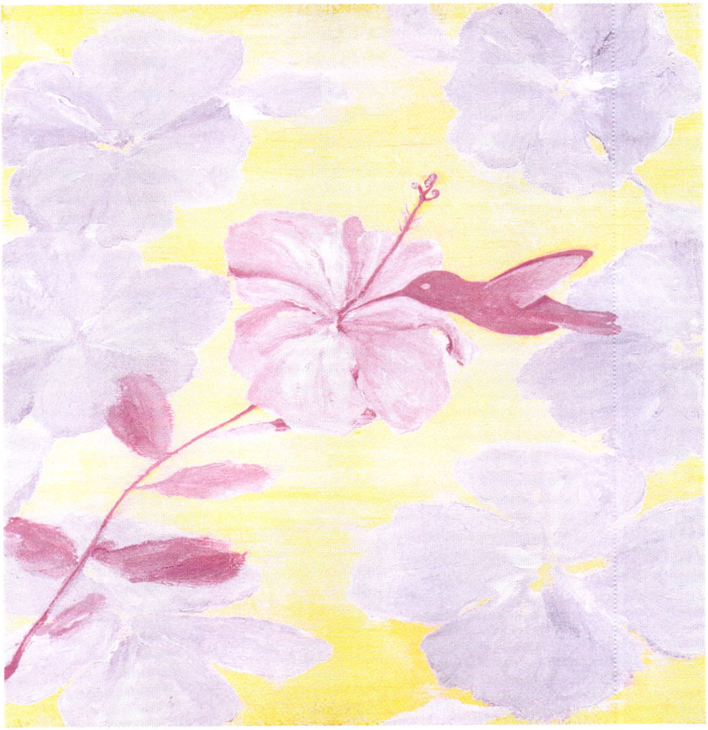

**Look at any of the pictures,**

and you will find areas of calm spreading out around it. Pictures like this don't make many demands at first. They're about things you like, things that are significant without insisting on being perceived. Glenn's work is aesthetically appealing, but if you look closer its conventionality is fragmented and accompanied by a composite group of historical companions. So what does it mean? What can we elicit from it once we have established our own fascination?

Something in the paintings is like the even, uninterrupted growth of things. It is the botanical imagery and structures that suggest this, of course. Flowers are mostly used as different orders of celebratory symbols, but they aren't necessarily revelatory or representative. They also embody a day-in, day-out, all-year-round sense of the present, of the reality of time. Flowers on the window sill are resident. They express tolerance and are susceptible to minute changes in light, humidity, and other forms of communication. Unlike the dead things that surround us, they are a responsive presence – whether they are subject to a pretty house or a pretty regimented garden, or are the kind that shoot out between concrete slabs in the pavement like polluted weeds. And if these flowers don't grow where they should (as it is often the case), the reason they're not eradicated could be because the gradual unfolding of their presence, from armoured seed to layered bud, decides the place of their growth and their more or less legitimate appearance of having been located somewhere. (These processes of uninterrupted sequences are reversible in Glenn's paintings; the cigarettes in the earlier paintings burn to ashes with the same vegetable determination as plants putting out their leaves).

There are many plants and flowers that figure as referents in Glenn's paintings. One such referent could be the dots of spring leaves in the Finnish painter Helene Schjerfbeck's **The Convalescent** from 1888, in which a little girl wrapped in blankets is recovering from an illness. Sitting in her wicker chair she stares at a twig in a mug. What stays with you is her tousled hair and the way she palpitates the twig, which bends towards her as if to return her blue-eyed gaze with a green one. The painting is seemingly an allegory of hope and days to come, but the girl's black sweater and the sheet that shrouds her body up to her armpits reduce her to a half-presence. This ambiguity of presence also flows through the motifs in Glenn's paintings; the ashtrays, purple flowers, patterns and portraits are precariously balanced – between the fullness of a proper name, for instance, and the mere outline of a face. This balance is the attempt to hold up or hold on to something fragile. A bit like the heavy paperweight on the convalescent's table: a weird, seemingly empty symbol enshrining in transparent glass what looks like a butterfly or a couple of flapping, purple petals.

## Take care of the world!

Glenn's paintings are a kind of interior, with the emphasis on the psychological dimension of the word. The placement and creation of the object in his paintings precedes the object's explanation and, in a sense, its sensation. Their appeal is that of the enchanted gaze you fix on a photo with out-of-sync colours that make you want to enter that photo's world because its aura is so soft and feel-good (like Jack Smith's slightly stoned performance documentation). It's a "Yes, that's what I want to feel like!" Something emotionally authentic is inserted between you and the object, a screen of the previously perceived and felt, and not quite present, a screen for prescribed pleasure. There is much emotional input in the paintings, but not a lot of information. These works aren't meaning cards. They are an effort to be sincere, whether based on primary or secondary experience, and they try to communicate the facts of inner time.

You might say they are a suggestive and often de-populated version of "the prelude or the refrain of movement, the promise of movement to come, or the echo of movement past,"[1] as Walter Sickert put it. As when you were on holiday in Greece and waited until returning to your hotel late at night, half drunk, to pick the hibiscus flowers you had spotted earlier in the hotel garden. You didn't want the hotel staff to catch you at it, and you placed them in the fridge overnight to keep them fresh. You made water-colours of them when you woke up. It may not seem like a big deal, but it means a lot.

Glenn seems to be interested in the pretty and intimate effects of identity. The concept of intimacy that he plays with could be the vernacular of the flowery textile samples he obtained from shops in Australian backwater towns. The stray aesthetic of these patterns is also the fibre in the texture of the "screen" and the images projected on it. But in Glenn's work the patterns are used strategically, in opposition to the specific appeal of the sources ("specific" because such aesthetic structures, like kitsch, only have limited and arbitrary sensational and intellectual applicability).

**Distraction in the social environment.**

The paintings seem preoccupied, distracted, because they never relate to an object directly. Even so, there is no doubt that the task of the paintings is positive. Their aim is to encourage the longevity of things beyond; the painted flower is never preferred to the real one, the painted hummingbird can't compete with the beating of wings. An object is favoured as a motif without being explicitly narrated: the stylized hummingbird, an ashtray, a long-chord telephone, a flower in a special vase. Other motifs are the result of fantastic manipulation, like the cigarette plants (are you growing too many cigarette butts? time to quit?), or the melancholic protraction of a situation, as in **Endless Cigarette** (come, let's take a cigarette break that goes on forever). The physical borders of the object are often dissolved because object and background are modulations of the same colour (painting as camouflage of the object); or the canvas and its motif are doubled in a symmetrical gesture (the mutual interest of two canvases in keeping reality at bay). Then there are fleeting glimpses of things on a scrambled background. Sometimes these airy-fairy markers are anchored in a black that isn't that easy to analyse; all the colours collapse into an almost palpable presence on a white wall.

If an ornament is something deprived of time, pure extent determined and stable, then Glenn's paintings are structured like ivy – a real plant that grows on surfaces, always looking for new places to find support, and occasionally stretching around the corner of a window or a mirror to settle on its own reflection. The paintings' form and presentation are like... well, like a flower: an isolated eruption.

## Could I love you till death do us part? Perhaps.

Can a telephone grow? Can an ashtray? Can a plant grow cigarette butts? Well, not in the neurological sense of the word. And conversely, with objects like the telephone and the ashtray there is no disintegration that doesn't relate to the breakdown of function. When you apply the notion of growth to things like these it must be taken to mean relocation, new constellations, re-signification in dry and scrubby paint. A micrology of figures of vulnerability; all the communication that can break and fall apart. Early feminist art reformulated traditional handicraft as a repressed art form that had been denigrated by patriarchy. And while flower painting has always been a deterritorialized art form reserved for those excluded from the all-male art schools, it has never really recovered from being a **Hausfrau** genre. But in a sense, Glenn's flower painting isn't about flower painting at all. As when Roland Barthes declared that he had spent May '68 not on the streets of Paris but painting watercolours at his mother's in the countryside, "the preferred occupation of 18th-century maidens". This didn't mean that Barthes rebuked the political; he merely opened it to the unexpected. Glenn's labour-intensive paintings are obviously of a different decorative order than old school feminist art, but one thing they have in common is that they are light years away from the pretension of modernist doxy, let alone the current postmodernist prolixity of bigger and faster artistic trends. According to popular convention and institutional expectation – and in opposition to expansive, painterly oomph – Glenn's canvases are a little undersized and awry. They convey signifiers that are neat and constrained, some of them whimsical, some of them so domestically straightforward you hardly identify them as "motifs" in **that** sense.

The motifs (even the fantastic ones and especially the portraits) are homely on one level, like padded oven gloves or pink, quilted carpets. And they're as light as glitter, a fast and modern way of expressing real emotion. The individuality of represented things has been reduced to a fleeting outline that acknowledges what is going on in the space in which those things are located. Likewise, their installation – scarce, like little islands – is telling. On these expanses of white walls, some of the paintings have the same silence and perversity as Luc Tuymans' work, but they lack its chill and terror. In Tuymans, an orchid can be an apocalypse. In Glenn's work we are somehow always close to the possible interruption and loss of what exists. Or, as he puts it in the title borrowed from a pop song, "Drive Carefully Darling".

**Loose brushwork, new traces.**

In Western art, botanical imagery tends to lead to ominous ideas and visions of decay (or frivolous a esthetics). It has been this way since swirls of Symbolist anxiety laced the water around Ophelia with petals. But perhaps true botanicity lies in a slowly evolving, freely flowing imagination that is simultaneously bound and unbound and that overgrows paradoxes and antagonisms? Because the images it spawns take place far away from what we usually consider to be defining representations and main events.

Symbolist or "decadent" art from the turn of the previous century held the human condition in a powerful, metaphorical grip. Glenn's signifiers aren't privileged ones that aim for the marrow of the zeitgeist. They are objects to be found at home, small banalities, though often rendered in decadent colours and rudimentary, nervous art nouveau wobble. You might say that the disposition of Glenn's paintings – his motif, conceptual strategies, and "technique", to use an old-fashioned term – is slightly obsessed, but it doesn't render the represented objects and people as more than they are, and the associations and fantasies they spur. Decadence means to allow yourself the luxury of worried, languorous introspection, and Glenn is probably on the introspective side, but it comes across as a necessity rather than a luxury. He confronts anxiety with humble signs that are preoccupied with their segment of reality. This is painting that is excited but is still careful with the housekeeping money. Even though each painting's "narration" or motif may be insignificant in the conventional sense, its rendition and presence is heartfelt: a quality intimated in its line, form, colour and composition. The signifiers are lighter than what their motive desire would be like if we could ever pin it down and represent it. This desire is real and ephemeral, and we are never given its point of departure. The paintings' motor is a force of gravity beneath the hummingbirds, cigarettes and disco flowers. For all their lightness, they represent the deadly serious struggle of a desire searching for its place in the world.

**Lars Bang Larsen**

1. Richard Shone: **Walter Sickert**, Phaidon Press, Oxford, 1988, p. 40

Pink and Brown, 2000

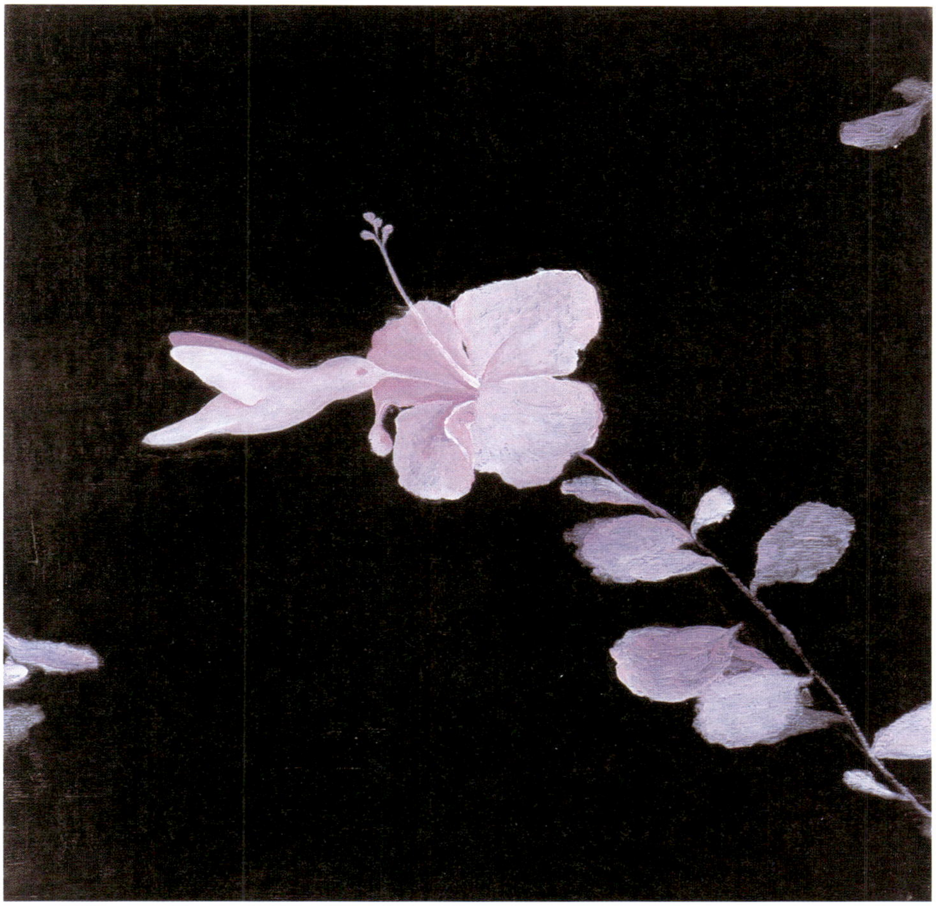

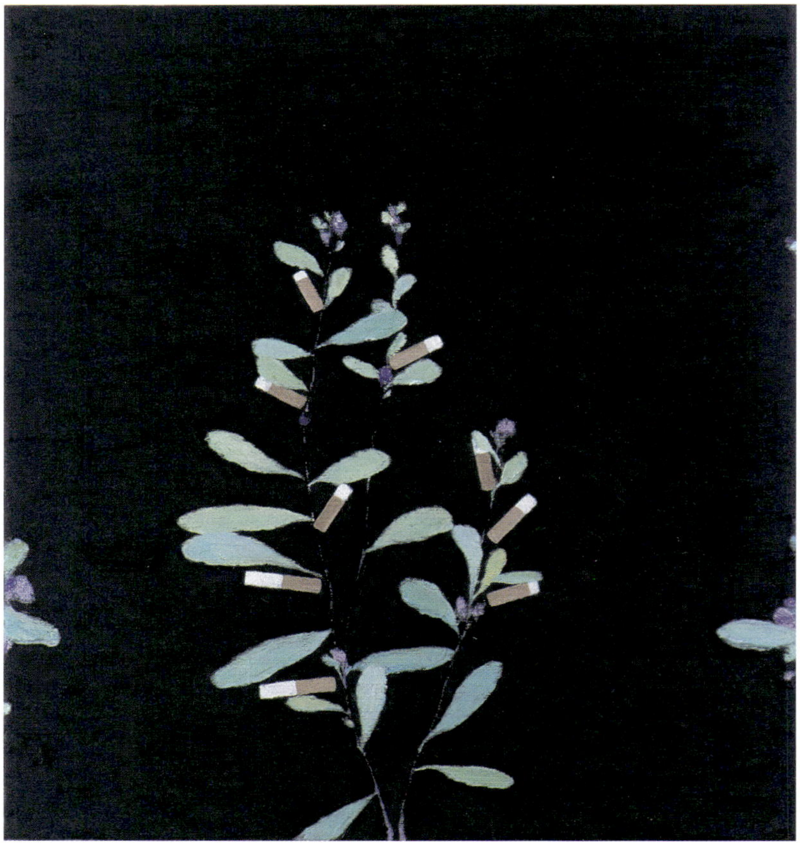

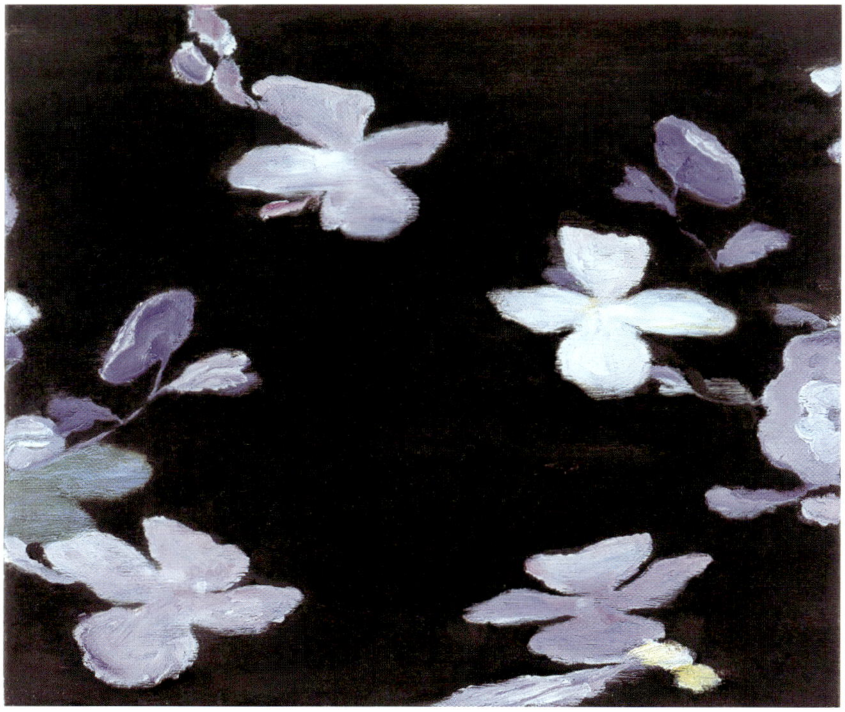

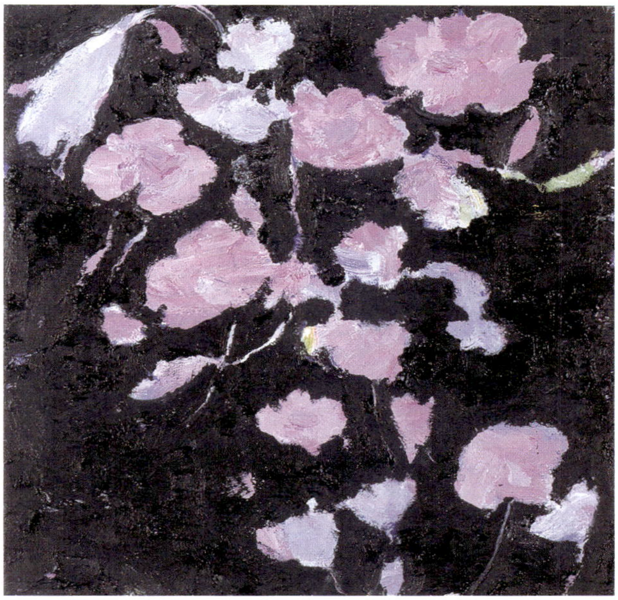

Flowers, 1999

Budding, 1999

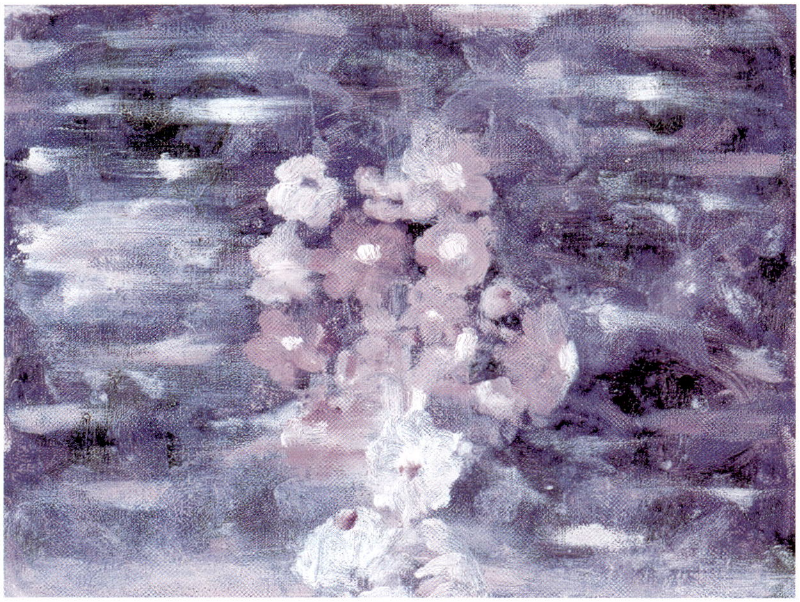



Disco Flowers, 1998

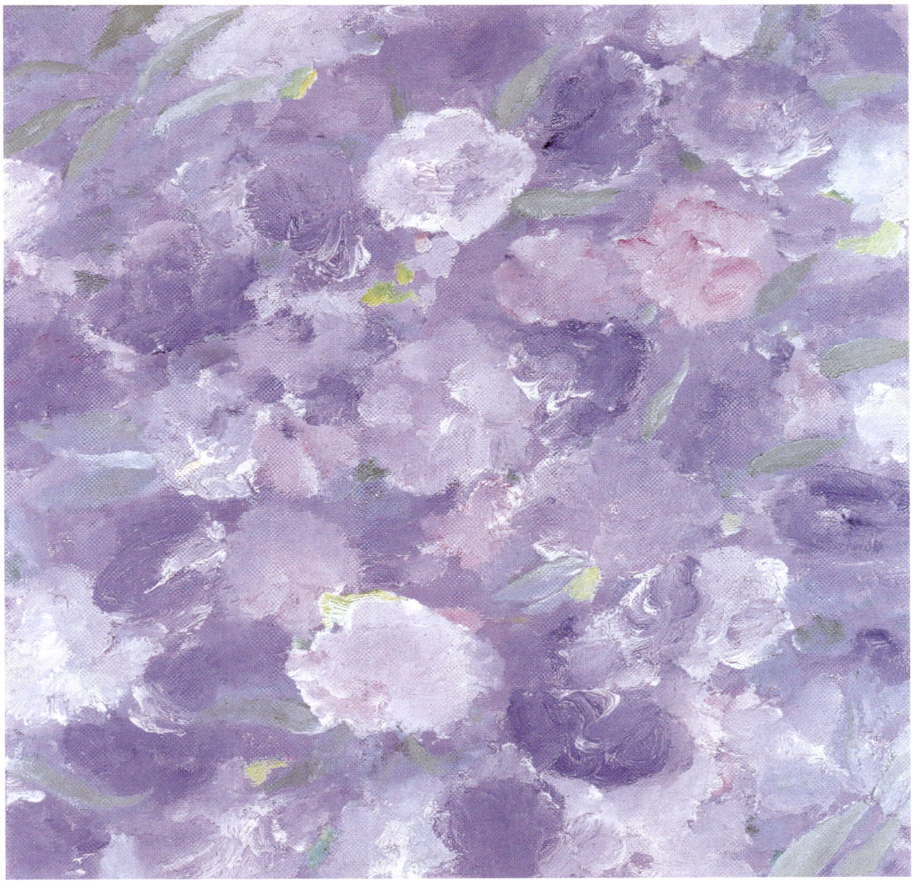

Purple Flowers, 1998

Flowers, 1998

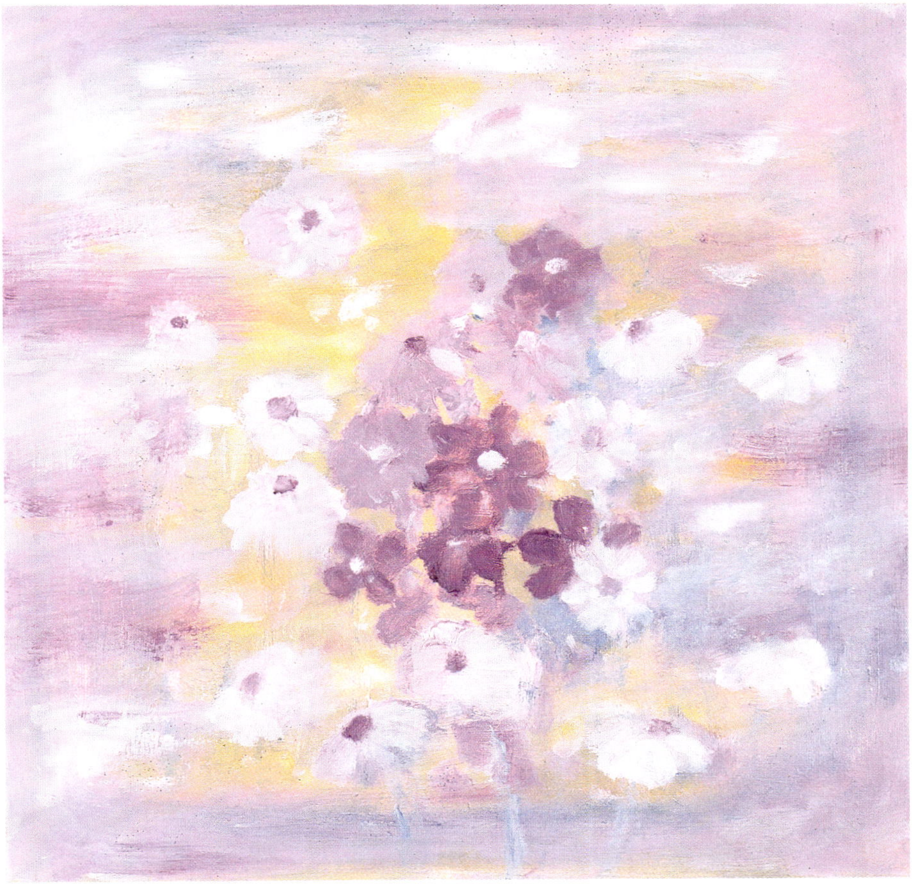

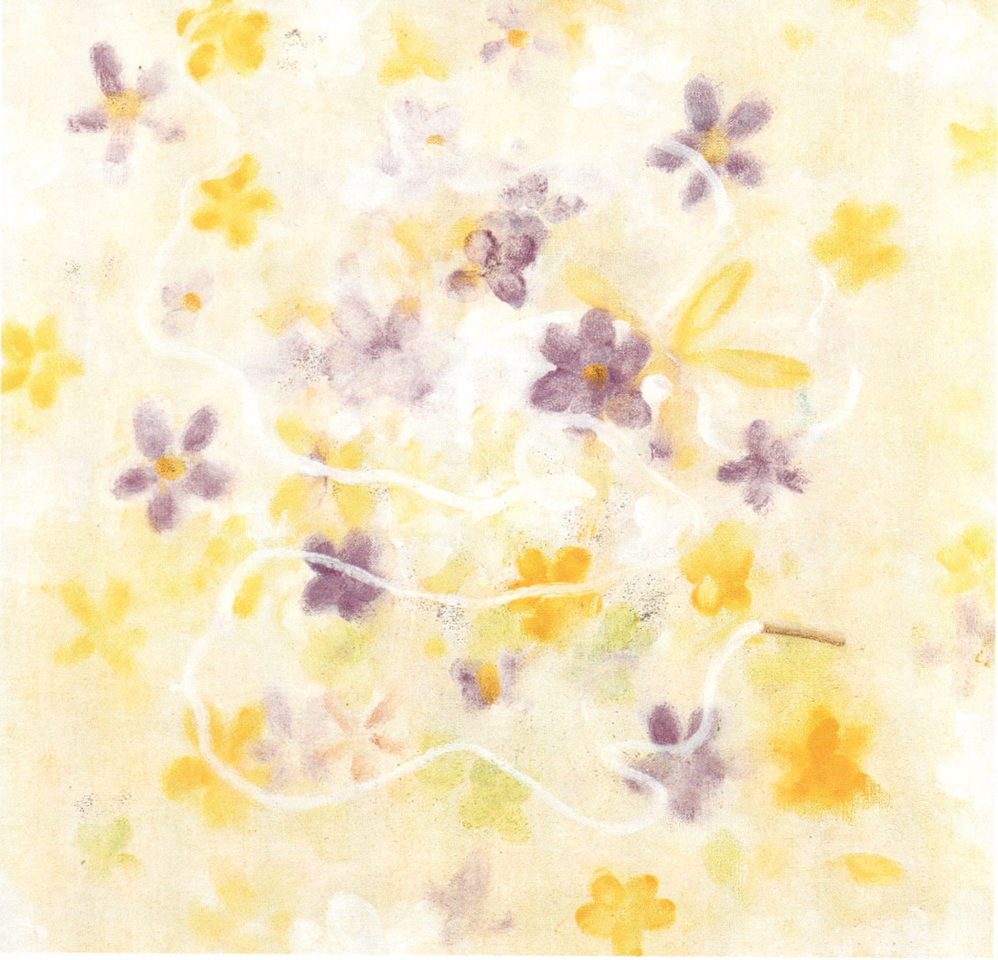



Endless Cigarette, 1997

Flowers, 1998

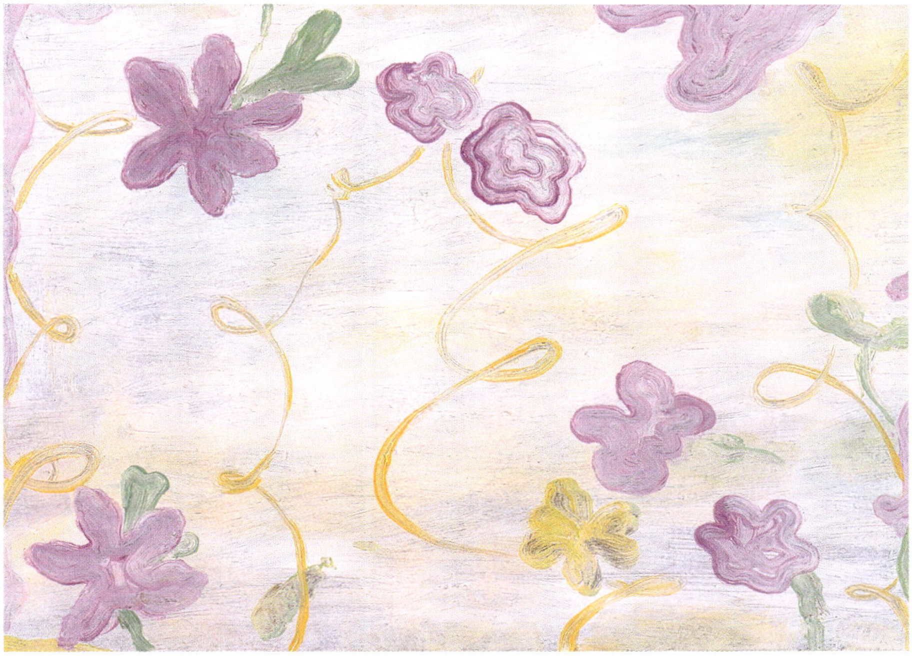

Roses, 2000

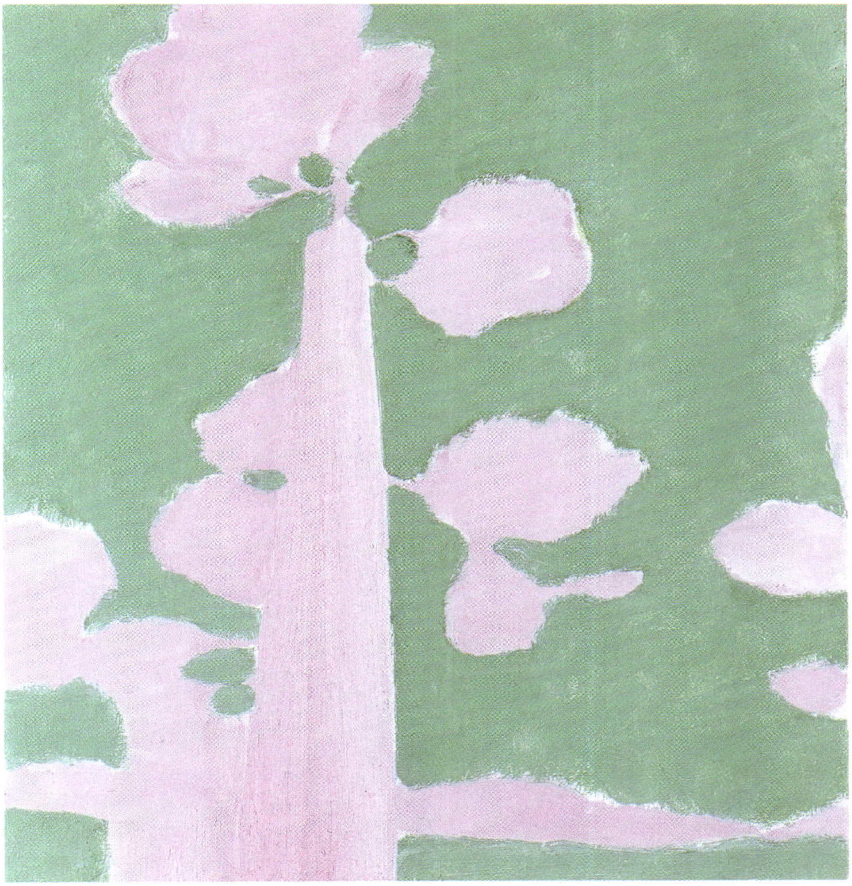

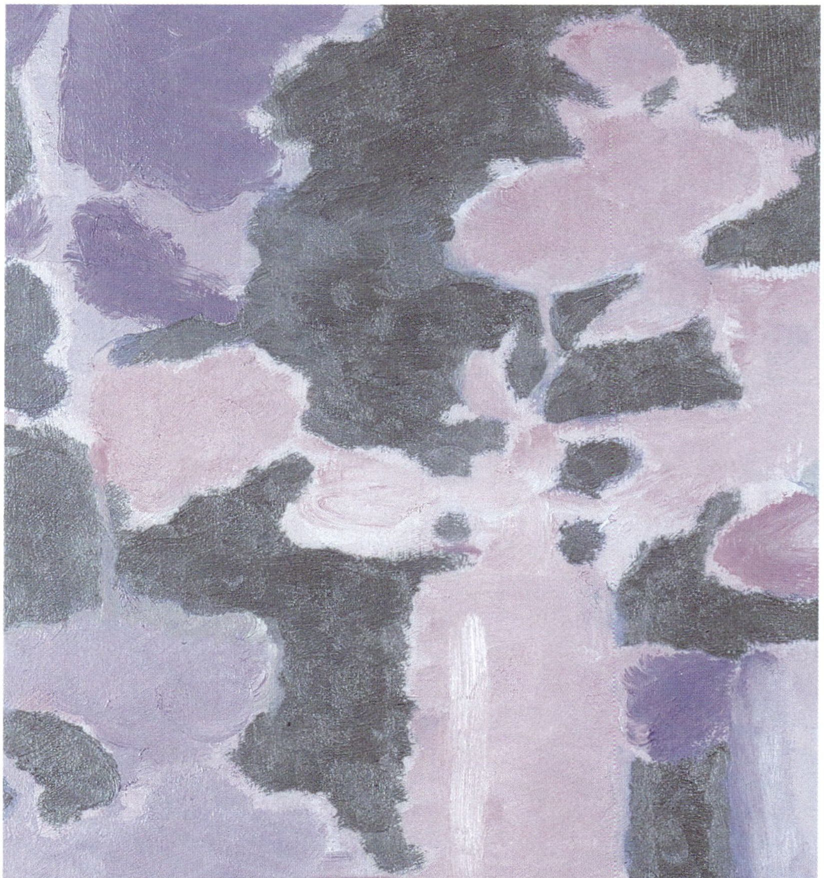

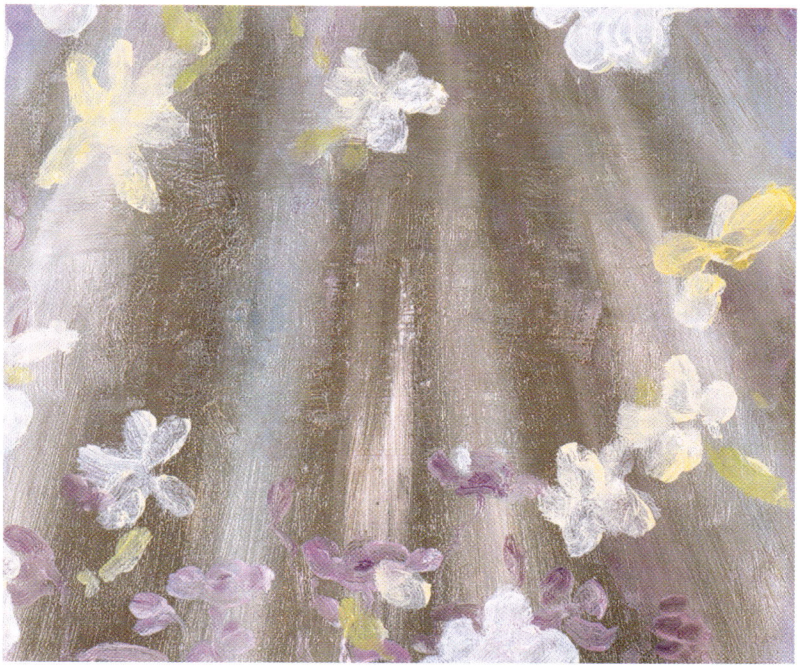

**Glenn Sorensen**

Born 1968 in Sydney, Australia

Lives and works in Malmö, Sweden

**Education**

| | |
|---|---|
| 1986-88 | City Art Institute, Sydney |
| 1990 | Helsinki Academy of Fine Arts, Helsinki |

**Solo Exhibitions**

| | |
|---|---|
| 2001 | Corvi-Mora, London |
| | Francesca Pia, Bern |
| | Galleria Raucci/Santamaria, Naples |
| 2000 | Annet Gelink Gallery, Amsterdam |
| | Hummingbirds and Ashtrays, Galleri Nicolai Wallner, Copenhagen |
| 1998 | F-rummet, Malmö Konstmuseum, Malmö |
| 1995 | I Don't Know Why I Feel Sick – Maybe I Got Out of Bed Too Quick, Galleri Nicolai Wallner, Copenhagen |
| 1994 | Welcome, Ynglingagatan 1, Stockholm |

**Group Exhibitions**

| | |
|---|---|
| 2001 | Extended Painting, Monica de Cardenas, Milan |
| | Drawings, Sommer Contemporary Art, Tel Aviv |
| 2000 | Premio Michetti, Museo Michetti, Pescara (Curator Gianni Romano) |
| | Corvi-Mora, London |
| | Painterly, 11th Vilnius Painting Triennial, Contemporary Art Centre, Vilnius |
| 1999 | Superiride, Galleria Raucci/ Santamaria, Naples |
| | Lè Grand Première Opening Show, Galleri Nicolai Wallner, Copenhagen |
| 1998 | Bokslut, Malmö Konstmuseum, Malmö |
| 1996 | Update, Turbinehallen, Copenhagen |
| 1995 | Ram, Portalen, Hudinge |
| | Atomic, Oberwelt, Stuttgart/Titanic, Turku (Curator Henrik Plenge Jakobsen) |

| | |
|---|---|
| 1994 | Project, Ynglingagatan 1, Stockholm |
| | Smells Like Teenspirit, Galleri Nicolai Wallner, Copenhagen |
| | No Vacancies, Hanauer Landstrasse 204, Frankfurt am Main |
| | Something´s Wrong, Nikolaj, Copenhagen |
| | Weirdos, Saga Basement, Copenhagen |

**Performances**

| | |
|---|---|
| 1995 | Warm Glow, Smart Show, Stockholm |
| | The Warm Affection Trip, Affiks, Lund |
| 1994 | New Reality Mix, Stockholm |

## Selected bibliography

Ela Caroli, 'Superiride, arte e ironia del profondo Nord', Corriere del Mezzogiorno, 1. December 1999

Simona Barucco, 'Superiride', Flash Art, N0. 219, Italian Edition, 1999

Stefania Zuliani, 'Mostra. Da trisorio e da Raucci e Santamaria', Il Mattino, 30. November 1999

Lisbeth Bonde, 'Kolobrier og Kniplinger', Information, 20. January 2000

Peter Michael Hornung 'Cigarettræer', Politiken, 21. January 2000

Jörn Ebner, 'Tiefer Griff in die Familienkiste', Frankfurter Allgemeine, 8. April 2000, no. 84

## List of works

(pag. 4)
Installation view
Annet Gelink Gallery, Amsterdam
2000

(pag. 5)
Installation view
Annet Gelink Gallery, Amsterdam
2000

(pag. 11)
Cigarette Plant
1999
Oil on canvas
41 x 33 cm
Private collection, London

(pag. 12)
Cigarette Plant
1999
Oil on canvas
45 x 38 cm
Collection Malmö Konstmuseum

(pag. 13)
Flowers
1998
Oil and glitter on canvas
32 x 40 cm
Collection Filippo Maggia, Varese

(pag. 15)
She Talks in her Sleep
1998-99
Oil on canvas
32 x 37 cm
Courtesy Galleri Nicolai Wallner, Copenhagen

(pag. 17)
You're the Only One
2000
Oil on canvas
37 x 38 cm
Courtesy Galleri Nicolai Wallner, Copenhagen

(pag. 18)
Jean
2000
Oil on canvas
35 x 35 cm
Collection B.J. van Egteren, Amsterdam

(pag. 19)
Purple Effect
1999
Oil on canvas
37 x 37 cm
Courtesy Galleri Nicolai Wallner, Copenhagen

(pag. 20)
Chrysanthemums
2000
Oil on canvas
40 x 35 cm
Courtesy Galleri Nicolai Wallner, Copenhagen

(pag. 21)
Drive Carefully Darling
2000
Oil on canvas
35 x 41 cm
Collection Erik van't Hoog, Amsterdam

(pag. 22)
Purple Vase of Flowers
2000
Oil on canvas
35 x 41 cm
Courtesy Galleri Nicolai Wallner, Copenhagen

(pag. 23)
Drive Carefully
1999
Oil on canvas
31 x 39 cm
Collection Nils Erik Gjerdevik, Copenhagen

(pag. 24)
Self-Portrait
1998
Oil on canvas
53 x 43 cm
Courtesy Galleria Raucci/Santamaria, Naples

(pag. 25)
Anna
1998
Oil on canvas
47 x 43 cm
Collection Francesco Annarumma, Angri

(pag. 27)
Waterfall
2000
Oil on canvas
40 x 36 cm
Private collection, London

(pag. 28)
Mushrooms
1998-99
Oil on canvas
30 x 30 cm
Collection Mino and Barbara Mazzoccato,
Montebelluna TV

(pag. 29)
Anna
2000
Oil on canvas
37 x 35 cm
Courtesy Galleri Nicolai Wallner, Copenhagen

(pag. 31)
Mauve Phone
2000
Oil on canvas
45 x 39 cm
Courtesy Annet Gelink Gallery, Amsterdam

(pag. 32)
Asleep in Front of Television
2000
Oil on canvas
40 x 34 cm
Collection Annet Gelink, Amsterdam

(pag. 33)
All Night Every Night
2000
Oil and glitter on canvas
36 x 35 cm
AKZO Nobel Art Foundation, Arnhem

(pag. 34)
Feeder
2000
Oil on canvas
36 x 40 cm
Courtesy Annet Gelink Gallery, Amsterdam

(pag. 35)
Hibiscuses
2000
Oil on canvas
35 x 35 cm
Courtesy Galleri Nicolai Wallner, Copenhagen

(pag. 36)
Pelargoniums
2000
Watercolour on paper
38 x 28.5 cm
Private collection, London

(pag. 36)
Hibiscuses
2000
Watercolour on paper
36 x 26 cm
Courtesy Corvi-Mora, London

(pag. 37)
Pelargoniums
2000
Watercolour on paper
38 x 28.5 cm
Courtesy Corvi-Mora, London

(pag. 37)
Hibiscus-mirror
2000
Watercolour on paper
36 x 26 cm
Private collection, London

(pag. 39)
Pink Hummingbirds
1999
Oil on canvas
37 x 35 cm
Collection Malmö Konstmuseum

(pag. 41)
Probleema
1997
Oil on canvas
35 x 27 cm
Collection Umberto Raucci and Carlo Santamaria, Naples

(pag. 42)
Ashtray 1/2
1997-98
Oil on canvas
55 x 55 cm
Collection Malmö Konstmuseum

(pag. 43)
Ashtray 2/2
1997
Oil on canvas
55 x 55 cm
Collection Malmö Konstmuseum

(pag. 45)
Four Ashtrays
1998-99
Oil on canvas
37 x 40 cm
Courtesy Galleri Nicolai Wallner, Copenhagen

(pag. 46/47)
Installation view
Hummingbirds and Ashtrays
2000
Galleri Nicolai Wallner, Copenhagen

(pag. 48/49)
Installation view Superiride
Galleria Raucci/Santamaria, Naples
Ashtrays 1/3, 2/3, 3/3
75 x 75 cm each
1999

(pag. 50)
My Mother-in-law´s Flowers
1999
Watercolour on paper
36 x 26 cm
Private collection, London

(pag. 50)
Flower and Cigarettes
1999
Watercolour on paper
36 x 25 cm
Courtesy Galleri Nicolai Wallner, Copenhagen

(pag. 51)
Flowers
1999
Watercolour on paper
26 x 36 cm
Private collection, London

(pag. 52/53)
Installation view
Hummingbirds and Ashtrays
2000
Galleri Nicolai Wallner, Copenhagen

(pag. 55)
Hummingbird
1999
Oil on canvas
33 x 31 cm
Private collection, Amsterdam

(pag. 63)
Pink and Brown
2000
Oil on canvas
41 x 41 cm
Private collection, Amsterdam

(pag. 64)
Night Light
2000
Oil on canvas
38 x 35 cm
Collection Martin van Zomeren, Amsterdam

(pag. 66)
Flowers
1999
Oil on canvas
32 x 37 cm
Collection Monica De Cardenas, Milan

(pag. 67)
Budding
1999
Oil on canvas
27 x 27 cm
Courtesy Galleri Nicolai Wallner, Copenhagen

(pag. 68)
Disco Flowers
1998
Oil on canvas
27 x 35 cm
Collection Peter Land, Copenhagen

(pag. 69)
Purple Flowers
1998
Oil on canvas
40 x 40 cm
Private collection, London

(pag. 71)
Flowers
1998
Oil and glitter on canvas
40 x 40 cm
Collection Francesca Pia, Bern

(pag. 72)
Endless Cigarette
1997
Oil on canvas
45 x 44 cm
Collection Piezzi-Iornini, Naples

(pag. 73)
Flowers
1998
Oil on canvas
50 x 47 cm
Courtesy Galleri Nicolai Wallner, Copenhagen

(pag. 75)
Lilly
1998
Oil on canvas
30 x 40 cm
The Speyer Family Collection, New York

(pag. 77)

Roses

2000

Oil on canvas

40 x 37 cm

Courtesy Galleri Nicolai Wallner, Copenhagen

(pag. 78)

Silver Day

2000

Oil on canvas

40 x 36 cm

Courtesy Corvi-Mora, London

(pag. 81)

Ray of Light

1998

Oil on canvas

30 x 35 cm

Collection Annet Gelink, Amsterdam

**Special thanks to**

Lars Bang Larsen
Tommaso Corvi-Mora
Annet Gelink
Jennifer Higgie
Erik van 't Hoog
Tony Manning
Jan Mol
Michiel Mol
Anne Marie Nuss
Umberto Raucci
Carlo Santamaria
Anna Sorensen
Gijs Stork
Nicolai Wallner
Tanja Wallroth

## Colophon

| | |
|---|---|
| Concept | Glenn Sorensen |
| Producer | Gijs Stork |
| Texts | Jennifer Higgie |
| | Lars Bang Larsen |
| Translation | Nancy Forest Flier |
| Design | Gracia Lebbink/Bregt Balk |
| Photography | Planet Foto/Bent Fryberg |
| | Ingrid Nilsson |
| | Marcus Leigh |
| | Messico |
| Printing | Drukkerij Die Keure, Brugge |
| Edition | 2000 |
| Published by | Artimo Foundation, 2001 |
| | Fokke Simonszstraat 8 |
| | 1017 TG Amsterdam |
| ® Copyright | Glenn Sorensen, |
| | the authors and Artimo |
| | Foundation, ® 2001 |
| ISBN | 90-75380-26-7 |
| Distribution | Idea Books |
| | Nieuwe Herengracht 11 |
| | 1011 RK Amsterdam, |
| | The Netherlands |
| | tel: +31 20 622 61 54 |
| | fax: +31 20 620 92 99 |